Melbourne Dreaming

SECOND EDITION

A GUIDE TO IMPORTANT PLACES OF THE PAST AND PRESENT

Meyer Eidelson

Aboriginal
Studies Press

Barak by Florence Ada Fuller, 1885.
State Library of Victoria, H24649.

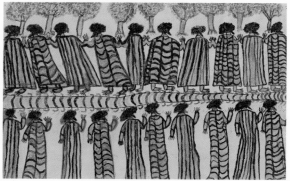

William Barak, Wurundjeri figures
in possum-skin cloaks. National
Gallery of Victoria, 1215A-5.

Dedicated to William Barak, Ngurungaeta (clan leader) of the Wurundjeri, who died at Coranderrk, Healesville in 1903. As a boy, he was present at the signing of John Batman's treaty (the Melbourne Treaty). An outstanding leader in the struggle for Aboriginal rights and justice, he guided his people with courage and wisdom through extraordinary times.

CONTENTS

ABOUT THE AUTHOR

Meyer Eidelson was born in Melbourne, has always lived there and plans to keep it that way. His love affair with the Melbourne landscape has been expressed through fifteen previously published books set in Melbourne. Most were produced to raise funds for environmental and historical organisations that cherish their city.

His parents were Holocaust survivors who arrived in Australia in 1949 after their extended families perished. This family history has strongly influenced Meyer's writings which explore identity, home and place as well as reconciliation. As a naturalist he believes that Aboriginal spiritual and ecological beliefs are the philosophy most attuned to the Australian landscape.

In the 1990s he worked for the Victorian state government for seven years in partnership with Aboriginal organisations to build self-managed services for Koorie elders across Victoria.

In 1997, he approached Aboriginal Affairs Victoria and traditional owners with the concept of creating the first guide book to Melbourne's Aboriginal places to improve awareness of Koorie heritage. The result was the first book of its kind, *The Melbourne Dreaming*, which later inspired *Aboriginal Sydney* and *Aboriginal Darwin*. Today Meyer is the owner of Melbournewalks.com which provides guided heritage activities across Melbourne.

ABOUT THIS BOOK

Melbourne Dreaming is both a guide book and social history of Melbourne, and the events and cultural traditions that have shaped local Aboriginal people's lives. It aims to show where to look to gain a better understanding of the rich heritage and complex culture of Aboriginal people in Melbourne both before and since colonisation.

It was first published in 1997. This is a completely updated and expanded edition.

Melbourne Dreaming provides practical information on visiting both historical and contemporary sites located in the city centre, surrounding suburbs and outer areas. Arranged into seven precincts, *Melbourne Dreaming* takes you to beaches, parklands, camping places, historical sites, exhibitions, cultural displays and buildings.

For Melbourne's Aboriginal people the landscape prior to European settlement over which we travel was the face of the divine — the imprint of the ancestral creation beings that shaped the landscape on their epic journeys. Exploring Melbourne's Aboriginal places is a way of paying respect to this sacred tradition while learning more about our shared and ancient history.

Sites include locations and traces of important places before European settlement in 1835 such as shell middens, scarred trees, wells, fish traps, mounds and quarries. Other sites describe critical events that occurred because of the impact of European settlement. More recent places are the focus of contemporary life. What these places share in common is that each illustrates an important part of the overall story of the first inhabitants, the Kulin.

Stories and photographs of some places of interest which have restricted access or cannot be visited have also been included.

Melbourne Dreaming is a step towards assisting visitors, local residents and students to understand the enormous economic, cultural, social and historical contributions of Aboriginal people to the city.

Terms

Since 1969, 'Koori' or 'Koorie' is a term used widely by Aboriginal people in southeast Australia to describe themselves and differentiate from other Aboriginal communities. The terms 'Kulin' (the people), 'wurrungs' (language groups) and 'Aboriginal people' are also used in this book.

Aboriginal languages are oral, not written, and thus spelt with many variations: for example, there are over sixty versions of 'Boon Wurrung'. Today organisations are encouraged to consult and develop protocols with local Aboriginal communities when deciding on appropriate names and spellings. We have chosen spelling for places and names that make meanings as clear as possible while also including some variations to acknowledge that different spellings are widely used today by diverse Koorie communities and others.

'This is a map of Port Phillip Bay and all the rivers that flow into it. The Southern Cross represents the Kulin nation. The swirling motion of water in Birrarung (the Yarra River) travels to Port Philllip Bay in the centre. The five circular shapes represent the five clans of the Kulin Nation: Dja Dja wurrung, Boon wurrung, Taun wurrung, Woi wurrung and Watha wurrung. The border represents the land of mountains and valleys around Birrarung and the conection of animal, land and water.'

**Mandy Nicholson
Wurundjeri**

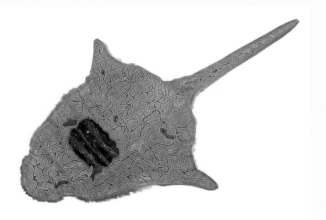

Mandy Nicholson, *Map of Port Phillip Bay*, paint, kangaroo skin, 128x80cm.

A glossary of words used in this book can be found at p. 137. An English translation is provided with the first use of the word. Language terms are italicised in the first instance and roman thereafter.

Woiwurrung (today Wurundjeri) and Boon Wurrung languages are estimated to have up to ninety three per cent of words in common. Both used the term *willam* meaning house, home or place, so willam is used to describe sites where people camped for purposes such as socialising, food gathering, performance, ceremonies, cultural business or trade.

Some historic accounts have been quoted verbatim to provide important insights into the past, while recognising the language used may include terms not in use today and which may be considered inappropriate to a contemporary reader.

Maps and descriptions are indicative only and should not be interpreted as a definitive statement about traditional or current land ownership or boundaries.

Getting around

Melbourne's suburbs and transportation radiate out from the CBD so our book starts with the city centre precinct and extends out to east, west, north and south. As a guide, the book provides practical information such as maps, street directory references, transport options, and facilities at the sites. Availability of facilities can change over time so check for up-to-date information before visiting. Bicycle and walking paths are included as most sites in this book are located on these trails.

For information about the many sites managed by Parks Victoria, contact:

Parks Victoria Information Centre
Tel: 13 19 63 or (03) 8627 4700
Email: info@parks.vic.gov.au
Web: www.parkweb.vic.gov.au

Public transport

For public transport information, including timetables, maps and fares, contact:

Public Transport Victoria
Tel: 1800 800 007 (6 am–midnight seven days a week)
Web: www.ptv.vic.gov.au.

Ticketing: the **myki** smartcard is required to travel on the city's metropolitan trains, trams and buses. They are available from main rail stations, retail outlets such as newsagents and convenience stores, online, and by phone: 13 69 54. Full fare myki cards can be purchased from myki machines at all metropolitan train stations as well as major tram and bus interchanges. For more information on myki, visit: http://ptv.vic.gov.au/tickets/myki

Bicycle

Melbourne is reasonably flat and well suited to cycling. There are many cycling routes throughout the metropolitan area. It is an ideal way to explore the city centre and inner suburban areas. Bicycles can be taken on suburban trains free of charge during off-peak times. Bicycle hire is available through many outlets including Melbourne Bike Share which is designed for easy hire and return around the inner city.

Car

To visit some sites, it may be more practical to travel by car. There are some toll roads in and around Melbourne. For more information on the location of these roads and paying tolls, contact:

CityLink
Tel: 13 14 50
Web: www.citylink.com.au

ABORIGINAL HERITAGE ACT

All Aboriginal cultural sites and relics in Victoria are protected by the *Aboriginal Heritage Act 2006* which includes Aboriginal artefacts. It is illegal to disturb or harm an Aboriginal site. Do not remove artefacts such as stones or shells from any site. Over 30,000 cultural places and objects are recorded on the Victorian Aboriginal Heritage Register maintained by Aboriginal Affairs Victoria.

Under the Act, traditional owners including registered Aboriginal parties play essential legal and management roles. The Victorian Aboriginal Heritage Council is the first decision-making body of its kind in Australia. Comprised of up to eleven traditional owners with extensive knowledge and experience, it ensures that Aboriginal people throughout Victoria play a central role in the protection and management of their heritage as well as advising state and local governments.

One of five rare Aboriginal earth rings at Sunbury. Courtesy Aboriginal Affairs Victoria.

ACKNOWLEDGMENTS

This publication could not have been produced without information provided by Aboriginal Affairs Victoria, staff of Parks Victoria, Victorian Aboriginal Corporation for Languages (VCAL), Sista Girl Productions, Museum of the West, National Gallery of Victoria, Aboriginal heritage staff of the Melbourne City Council, National Parks Victoria and the City of Port Phillip, Melbourne Museum's Bunjilaka Centre, Phil Wierzbowski of Coastcare Victoria, Baluk Arts, Pamela Pedersen and many others too numerous to mention. The personal assistance of Amanda Palmer was essential to complete the book.

I particularly thank Carolyn Briggs of the Boon Wurrung Foundation, Darren Griffen, Doreen Garvey-Wandin and Stephen Fiyalko of the Wurundjeri Tribe Land Cultural Heritage Council Inc and the Victorian Aboriginal Heritage Council for providing access to the Victorian Aboriginal Heritage Register.

I am grateful to Judy Williams, the Koorie Heritage Trust Librarian who recommended reprinting the book, and for the assistance of Bill Nicholson and Bill Nicholson Senior of the Wurundjeri Council.

We are fortunate in Victoria to have many outstanding researchers and writers on Aboriginal history whose publications have assisted in background research for this guide book. In this respect I 'stand on the shoulders of giants' such as Jim Berg, Vicki Couzens, Ian Clark, Richard Broome, Gary Presland, Marie Fels, Michael Cannon, Isabel McBryde, Michael Christie, Diane Barwick and Megan Goulding, to name just a few.

Since 1991, the reconciliation movement has substantially increased the involvement of public groups in Indigenous issues. Many local governments through Reconciliation Action Plans have commissioned groundbreaking research to create knowledge trails in consultation with

Indigenous communities. I am especially grateful to the cities of Stonnington, Bayside and Yarra, particularly Peter Redden, Anthony Jacobs, Daniel Ducrou and Aldo Malavisi. I have also included pathways created by the University of Melbourne and RMIT University Bundoora. I commend their commitment to the reconciliation cause: 'In all things — respect!'

ACKNOWLEDGMENTS (1997 EDITION)

This publication could not have been produced without the assistance, knowledge, and permission of the Wurundjeri people. The Wurundjeri are traditional custodians of most of the Melbourne metropolitan region. Their ancestors were among the tribes of Aboriginal people who inhabited this region for many thousands of years. The Wurundjeri have contributed a great deal of detailed information to this book. I am especially grateful for the assistance of Mr Bill Nicholson. Special thanks are also due to the Minister for Aboriginal Affairs, the Honourable Ann Henderson MP, who shares the vision of increasing community awareness of Victoria's Aboriginal heritage and who approved the funding for the preparation of the manuscript. While many people were involved in the project, it was Mr Terry Garwood, at that time Director of Aboriginal Affairs Victoria, who provided the necessary direction to ensure the successful outcome of the project. Numerous staff at Aboriginal Affairs Victoria also provided their expertise. The advice and information provided by officers of Parks Victoria, the Public Records Office, Melbourne, the Royal Historical Society, and numerous local government offices and private individuals were also of great assistance.

INTRODUCTION

The variety and number of Aboriginal places that still exist in a modern city like Melbourne are a surprise to many. Most people are unaware of these important locations even in iconic destinations such as the Royal Botanic Gardens, Southbank, the University of Melbourne and the Melbourne Cricket Ground. These sites demonstrate how Aboriginal history is an intrinsic part of the city's make-up as well as our nation's.

Every place tells a story, a chapter in the epic saga of Melbourne's first inhabitants, the Kulin nation or confederacy. To visit these sites is to begin a journey of understanding of the astonishing achievements of a people for whom Melbourne has been home since Bunjil, the great ancestor spirit of the wedge-tailed eagle, created their laws and lands. Archaeological evidence indicates occupation for at least 30,000 years in Melbourne's west. The courage of the Kulin ancestors brought them to this continent in the world's first great sea crossing perhaps 50,000 years ago. Their ingenuity and spiritual practice have enabled their survival through millennia of drought, ice age, volcanic eruption, earthquake and the flooding of their lands that created *Nairm* (Port Phillip Bay).

Perhaps their greatest challenge, after approximately 1600 generations, was the invasion by *ngamudji* (European settlers) of their lands. By 1835 when the settlers had reached Melbourne, about half the population may have already died as a result of smallpox epidemics spreading from northern Australia. Twenty years later Kulin numbers had fallen a further ninety per cent due to disease, dispossession and brutality.

The Kulin nation

The traditional owners that shared the Melbourne area were the Woiwurrung (today known as the Wurundjeri) and the

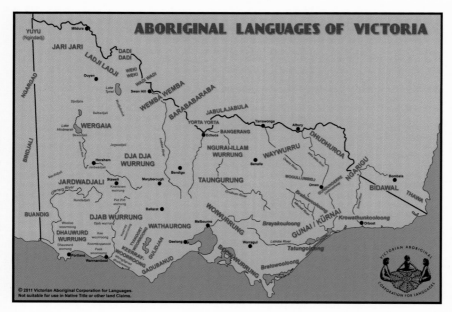

Map of languages group in the Melbourne/Port Phillip Bay area. This map was produced from information available at the time of printing. This map is not suitable for native title claims. Victorian Aboriginal Corporation for Languages.

Boon Wurrung peoples. They were part of the Kulin nation which comprised five related groups that shared similar languages. These *wurrungs* (language groups) were part of about thirty groups in Victoria, numbering an estimated 60,000 people before Europeans arrived.

Melbourne was a central location where the wurrungs met regularly for social and ceremonial gatherings, trade, initiation, marriage, and law business in places such as Southbank, *Tromgin* (the site of today's Royal Botanic Gardens), Yarra Bend, and Bulleen. Wurrungs were made up of clans or smaller landowning groups. At the time of European settlement, the six Boon Wurrung clans were recorded as claiming the coastal lands around Port Phillip Bay west to the Werribee River as well as Mornington Peninsula and Westernport as far as Wilsons Promontory. The four Woiwurrung clans (today represented by the Wurundjeri people) were recorded as occupying the Yarra River and Maribyrnong watersheds. The three other wurrungs are the Wathaurong (Wathawurrung) west of the Werribee River and the Dja Dja Wurrung (Djadjawurrung) and Taungurong (Daungwurrung), located north and northwest of the Great Dividing Range.

All members in a clan shared the same 'moiety' or totem, either *bunjil* (wedge-tailed eagle) or *waa* (crow) moiety. Marriage took place between people of opposite moieties so partners were found from other clans. The intricate kinship networks meant that during the year, clan members were often found visiting other estates. Clan members were hunter–gatherers, travelling regularly in smaller 'bands' throughout their estates on a seasonal basis to manage their country and harvest animals, reptiles, birds and eggs, shellfish and eels, wattle gum, and plants such as roots from a wide variety of landscapes such as the foreshore, wetlands, woodlands and hills. They developed highly efficient and lightweight tools as well as husbandry methods such as the use of fire to regenerate food plants and increase grazing lands for larger animals. They gathered sufficient food in just four to five hours per day, leaving plenty of time for important spiritual, ceremonial and family obligations.

The Yarra River around today's city centre was marked by lakes, billabong, swamps and lagoons, with abundant resources such as animals, plants, ducks, fish and vegetables. A rocky basalt ledge or waterfall at the site of today's Queens Bridge (city centre) was a central meeting place for the tribes as well as a 'bridge' to cross the river. Importantly, it separated upriver fresh water from downstream salt water. In 1835, this freshwater source was the impetus for the choice of place for a British colony destined to become the world's fastest growing metropolis.

First impact

On 15 February 1802, the *Lady Nelson* was the first ship to enter Port Phillip Bay. In October the following year, British colonists arrived to establish a penal colony near Sorrento but they found the water supply inadequate and the Boon Wurrung hostile. A few months later, they departed to found a settlement at Hobart, Van Diemen's Land (later renamed Tasmania), leaving behind escaped convict, William Buckley.

'My old ones tell me my spirit belongs here.'

**Joy Wandin Murphy
Wurundjeri**

Thirty-two years later, the settlers returned, seeking cheap land to grow Australian wool which was now fetching record prices in Britain. On 6 June 1835, John Batman, representing Tasmanian pastoralists, claimed to have signed a treaty with eight 'chiefs' of the Port Phillip tribes to purchase 600,000 acres of land in payment for £200 worth of beads, mirrors, clothing and axes. He boasted about his acquisition in a Launceston hotel. The publican, John Fawkner, was paying close attention and purchased the schooner, *Enterprize*, which arrived on the Yarra River at the site of today's Queens Bridge on 30 August 1835.

The collaboration of the settlers and the Kulin of Melbourne in the first year is fascinating. The small party of settlers wanted safe access to pastures. The Melbourne clans accepted, at face value, these new allies who swore friendship and promised new technologies such as iron, horses and weapons in return for being guests on their land. Their alliance was sealed by a *Tanderrum* ceremony of hospitality, friendship and ritual exchange of gifts. Derrimut, a Boon Wurrung *Arweet* (clan leader), even warned the settlers of an impending attack by hostile clans.

However, a few months later, the New South Wales colonial government declared the treaty invalid. It was the British, not the Kulin, who would have sovereignty over land and would profit from its lease or sale. Furthermore, the British released all settlers from the restrictions that bound them near settlements such as Sydney. Within five years more Aboriginal land in Australia was seized by settlers than in the previous fifty. By 1840, 4000 Europeans had flooded into Melbourne and 700,000 sheep were grazing on Aboriginal land. Two years later there were 1.4 million sheep in Victoria (called the Port Phillip District of New South Wales before separation from NSW in 1851).

These newer arrivals had little concept of treaty or mutual obligation. Relations became tense and then aggressive as the Kulin found their sacred lands usurped, their waterholes seized and their food sources destroyed by stock. Their economic, religious, social and cultural lives as well as their freedom of movement was disrupted. They often had little alternatives but to 'steal' stock and potatoes to feed their families and the settlers' reactions were often swift and violent. By 1839, hundreds of Kulin were regularly congregating in Melbourne seeking food, blankets and medical treatment, rapidly becoming refugees in their own country. Melbourne's medical officer warned of possible extinction after assessing Kulin sick with syphilis, typhus, bronchial disease, dysentery and tuberculosis.

The Aboriginal Protectorate

In 1839, the British government, fearing a repeat of the near-genocide of Aboriginal people in Tasmania in the 1820s, announced an Aboriginal Protectorate in Victoria with George Robinson as Chief Protector and four Assistant Protectors in order to: 'Civilise the Aboriginal residents, to teach them

Drawing on Bark (European man being speared), Pyramid Hill region, 1843. Sketch by George Robinson. State Library of New South Wales, A7039/8, vol 18, pt 8, p. 72.

'Blackfellows all about say that no good have them pickaninneys [children] now, no country for blackfellows like long time ago.' —

Billibellary, Woiwurrung clan leader, 1843.

agriculture, house-building and other white endeavours, to educate them to a settled European lifestyle and to convert them to Christianity.' Other attempted solutions included Aboriginal reserves, ration depots, mission schools and the Native Police Corps.

These humanitarian efforts failed. The Aboriginal economy involved movement across their territories for sustainable land management and to meet their kinship and religious responsibilities based on land as a sacred creation. The British, who believed their culture was superior, insisted on the adoption of Christianity and their system of fixed property and agriculture which offered the Kulin dependency, starvation and the loss of their traditional customs and beliefs.

The settlers never accepted that the Kulin preferred their own religion, economy, law, education and medicine, which were thousands of years old. As Assistant Protector William Thomas described, 'they have chiefs, doctors, counsellors, warriors, dreamers &c., who form a kind of aristocracy, yet these are in no way a burden to the community. The chiefs govern, doctors cure, counsellors advise, warriors fight, without pay.'

The British claimed that Aboriginal people were equal before the law yet they were arrested and held for trial without warrant, were unable to testify in court in their own and others' defence, and their lands were sold without permission or compensation. Reserves were established to provide 'homes' for displaced Aboriginal people and, according to the dominant European view of the time, a temporary measure until the Aboriginal race 'died out'.

By the 1840s, there was widespread resistance by the Kulin in frontier areas outside Melbourne but ultimately it proved futile against guns, horses and soldiers in a landscape with few places of retreat. The birth rate also dropped dramatically.

The only lasting contribution of the Protectorate, which closed in 1849, was their extensive journals and reports which today provide some of the most detailed descriptions of early Aboriginal life in Australia.

ACKNOWLEDGING A FAILED PROTECTOR

William Thomas was the Assistant Protector assigned to Melbourne, Westernport and Gippsland. His many reports, diaries and sketches provide vivid descriptions of early Aboriginal life as well as people such as Billibellary, Yoni Yonka, Matilda, Benbow, Kitty and Windberry. He failed as a Protector and Guardian as most of Melbourne's Aboriginal population died on his watch. He was frequently criticised by his employer Chief Protector George Robinson, the colonial authorities and the settlers.

Despite these challenges, Thomas remained a determined advocate for the Aboriginal cause and respectful of their leaders. His diaries show how this dedicated and eccentric man travelled constantly with the Melbourne wurrungs over their country, distributing food, blankets and medicine, teaching, recording, berating, despairing, mediating, attending burials, sermonising, but always trying to understand them. He almost died from exposure, assault and drowning but he did not give up. Many Kulin called him *Marminata* (Good Father) because Thomas was family to the Kulin and they were family to Thomas. He was unpopular in white society but ultimately it was Thomas, not his critics, who was right. He petitioned the government for Aboriginal self-determination, land tenure, financial compensation, law reform and limits to development 150 years before the reconciliation movement. If the government of the day had heeded his advice, it is possible, if only just, that history may have told a different story.

William Thomas, c.1860. State Library of Victoria, H2002.87.

Post-1851

The Gold Rush in 1851 saw the non-Aboriginal population increase seven times in the next decade. Any hope of Aboriginal control over their lands was swept away in a tidal wave of immigration. William Thomas reported that between 1835 and 1857 the Aboriginal population in Melbourne dropped from 350 to 28. In 1863, after the successful lobbying of Woiwurrung leaders and their supporter John Green, Coranderrk Aboriginal Station near Healesville was gazetted. It was an opportunity for the Woiwurrung and others to establish their own farming community and show the settlers they could live successfully this way. Many other Aboriginal people later moved to Coranderrk.

Initially, the community successfully cultivated hops, grew food for themselves and sold traditional handcrafts to tourists. However, this was later undermined by a faction within the Board of the Protection of Aborigines which was aligned with landowner interests. The Coranderrk residents, under the leadership of William Barak, campaigned to save the station and overturn management changes that eroded their independence and self reliance. They made direct representations to the government and wrote letters to the newspapers explaining their plight. They had several non-Aboriginal supporters — notably Mrs Anne Bonn who later became one of the humanitarian members of the Board. Their public campaign led to a parliamentary inquiry into the running of Coranderrk Station, held in 1881. It was the only inquiry of its kind in colonial Victoria. It was also unique in that it allowed Aboriginal people to testify.

The *Aboriginal Protection Act 1869* (Vic) gave powers to the Board for the Protection of Aborigines to determine where the Kulin could live and work as well as the ability to remove children if they were considered neglected. The attitude of settlers towards Aborigines was changing. The Aboriginal race was not 'dying out' as they first thought and the settlers were impatient to use the land set aside as Aboriginal reserves.

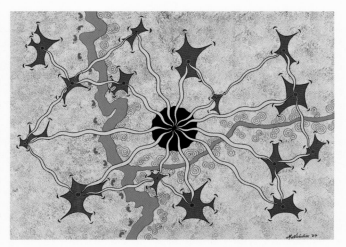

Mandy Nicholson, *Coranderrk*, 2004, acrylic board, 56.5x75cm. Koorie Heritage Trust, AH3419.

'Coranderrk, the black circle in the centre represents darkness, confusion, removal from home and family. Culture is depicted by campfires with the smoke connecting all the family groups. Even though the people at Coranderrk were told not to practice their 'savage and uncivilised' culture, they still had a strong connection to it. … The campfires (culture) didn't glow as bright. After they left the reserve the people went back to their Country and the campfire (culture) glowed strongly again.'

**Mandy Nicholson
Wurundjeri**

In 1886, the 'Half-caste' Act went further, ejecting those of 'mixed descent' between fourteen and thirty-four years of age from the missions to force their assimilation into the white population, despite well organised protests by the Coranderrk community under the leadership of William Barak and others.

The Act effectively broke up Koorie communities across Victoria and five of the six reserves were closed. It also undermined Aboriginal identity. For example, thirteen-year old-boys were apprenticed out and girls were placed into the service of white families, while 'neglected' children were transferred to white orphanages. Many never returned to the stations or their families.

Koories from these reserves were forced into an unwelcoming non-Aboriginal society where they were discriminated against. They found it hard to get work and housing, and many struggled to survive. Some chose to deny their origins and raised their children without telling them about their Aboriginal ancestry.

William Cooper, 1861–1941. Alick Jackomos collection, AIATSIS.

Revival

In 1932, Aboriginal community leader and political activist William Cooper and others established the Australian Aborigines' League to push for citizenship rights. They petitioned King George V and then Australian Prime Minister Joseph Lyons and announced a National Day of Mourning on Australia Day in 1938. Community leaders across Australia were inspired to create politically active organisations in the following decades such as the Aborigines Advancement League in 1957 and other Aboriginal-led health, housing, legal, media, sporting and community services. The 1967 Referendum was a watershed with 90.77 per cent of votes supporting Commonwealth power to legislate with respect to all Aboriginal people and to include them in the census with other Australians.

While the 1960s was a very important period where Aboriginal people achieved greater rights to citizenship, equal pay and financial assistance, they continued to push for equality and improvements including land rights and recognition of cultural heritage.

Today

Aboriginal culture has become an important part of Melbourne's political, economic, and creative life with a wide range of organisations including the Koorie Heritage Trust, 3KND (Kool n Deadly) Radio, Bunjilaka Centre, ILBIJERRI Theatre Company and many Aboriginal service organisations. Melbourne's traditional owners also play essential community and legal roles in the management of cultural places and objects. Reconciliation has become a key goal for state and local governments and many businesses and educational and community organisations.

From a traumatic past, Melbourne's Koories have made an inspirational revival through hard-fought struggles for social justice, legal reform, representation and self-managed organisations. Today there are almost 15,000 Aboriginal residents of Melbourne, many with achievements in fields as diverse as academia, health, media, music, art, sport and social services.

CITY CENTRE & SURROUNDS

The City of Melbourne covers 37.6 square kilometres and its economic, sporting and cultural centre is located within the city centre (CBD). Approximately 100,000 people from a wide range of cultures and backgrounds live in the City of Melbourne municipality which includes the inner suburbs of Carlton, Parkville, North Melbourne, Kensington, Docklands, Southbank and South Yarra.

This precinct was also once a central willam for people of the Kulin nation or confederacy. Today, the heart of the city with its gardens, historic buildings, galleries and museums, provides an excellent starting point to learn about Melbourne's Aboriginal heritage.

Sites 1–11 are all located within a 3.5 kilometre radius of the city centre (Bourke Street) [see map next page]. Parking can be difficult so the most convenient way of reaching these sites once you are in the city is often by public transport, bicycle or on foot.

View of Southbank from across the Yarra River — the River Yarra (Rainbow) Pedestrian Bridge is in the foreground. Photograph by Peter Dunphy, courtesy Tourism Victoria.

SITES

1. Birrarung (Yarra) Art and Heritage Walk
   Of Interest: Yarra Yarra Falls
2. Indigenous art collection
3. Koorie Heritage Trust
4. Freedom fighters execution site
5. Old Melbourne Cemetery site
6. Bunjilaka Cultural Centre
7. Billibellary's Walk
8. Fitzroy Gardens scarred tree
9. Melbourne Cricket Ground
10. Kings Domain Resting Place
11. Royal Botanic Gardens Aborigianl reserve site and Aboriginal heritage walk

CITY CENTRE & SURROUNDS

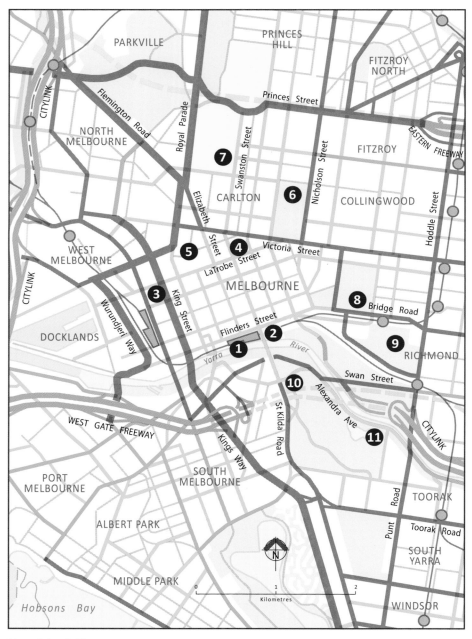

Map of sites 1–11.

The city centre is based on a very compact and accessible grid or 'golden mile' with trams on most main streets. Flinders Street Station is the main train terminus at the corner of Swanston and Flinders Streets. Southern Cross Station at the intersection of Bourke and Spencer Streets is the second main rail station and the key hub for country services.

A free City Circle Tram runs around the perimeter of the city centre every twelve minutes in both directions on most days of the year. A light rail tram service (numbers 96 and 109) travels to the popular tourist destinations of St Kilda and Port Melbourne (Beacon Cove). A free Melbourne Visitor Shuttle tourist bus operates daily every thirty minutes from Federation Square and travels to thirteen key inner city locations. Travellers can get off and on at any stop.

The CBD Melbourne Mobility Map, indicating wheelchair accessible and disability toilets, transport, parking, travellers aid and other services, is available from the Visitors Centre at Federation Square, the City of Melbourne on (03) 9658 9658 or the internet.

Most of Melbourne's shared use bicycle and pedestrian trails connect to the city centre. Many follow similar routes along the waterways used by Aboriginal clans during their seasonal travels. Most of the precincts in this book can therefore be reached via the Yarra Trail (city centre and east), Bayside Trail (south), Maribyrnong River Trail (west) and the Merri Creek Trail (north). TravelSmart maps of bike routes are available from Federation Square Visitors Centre or can be downloaded from the internet.

GETTING THERE

Public Transport: For information on services including how to connect to a destination, telephone 1800 800 007 from 6am to midnight daily or visit ptv.vic.gov.au.

Cycling and walking: Fifty bike share docking stations are located throughout the city centre, including Federation Square, where bikes can be hired cheaply and returned to any station. Instructions, maps and a free phone app can be downloaded from www.melbournebikeshare.com.au.

Birrarung Willam (River Camp), Birrarung Marr Park.
Photograph by Hari Ho.

DESCRIPTION
A three kilometre heritage walk that explores many Aboriginal art installations and sites of historic significance along Federation Square and Southbank.

LOCATION
Starting from Federation Square, Flinders Street. Melway: 1B Q10.

TIME 90 minutes.

FACILITIES
Toilets (wheelchair accessible) are available on the route at Federation Square, the National Galley of Victoria and the Immigration Museum.

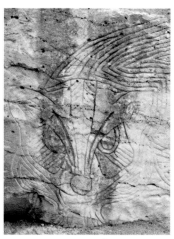

Rock engraving, *Birrarung Willam* installation. Photograph by Hari Ho.

SITE 1
Birrarung (Yarra) Art and Heritage Walk

Aboriginal people called Melbourne's river *Birrarung* but through a misunderstanding, British settlers called it the Yarra (see p. 11). The river is the dominant natural feature of the city centre and runs 242 kilometres from its source at Mt Baw Baw in the Yarra Ranges National Park to its mouth at the head of Port Phillip Bay. For Aboriginal people of the Kulin confederacy, it was a source of life carved into the landscape by the ancestral creator Bunjil, the wedge-tailed eagle. It was the Dreaming trail they followed and camped beside through countless seasons.

The river was the reason British settlers chose to settle here in 1835. Unfortunately, the city turned its back on the river in the mid-1800s when it was contaminated by pollution from industry and the docks. However, since the 1990s, Melbourne has re-embraced the river with enthusiasm, creating the Southbank arts and leisure precincts as well as the new suburb of Docklands. A new park, Birrarung Marr, meaning 'river of mist' has also been created adjoining Federation Square.

Melbourne's artists, designers and architects have expressed their pride in the city's Aboriginal heritage through creative sculptures, installations and structures along the river. Stroll along the waterway and experience how the best of modern Melbourne is married to an ancient past. The route includes heritage markers, Southgate and South Wharf areas, Melbourne Aquarium, Immigration Museum, Melbourne Convention Centre and Docklands (see suggested route right). Note that the walk is a collection of places within a three kilometre span and is not a set trail.

A. Nearamnew, Federation Square Plaza

The plaza, made from hundreds of thousands of Kimberley sandstone cobbles, is designed as a large artwork based on an 1860 Aboriginal bark painting depicting a whorl of water. The name *Nearamnew* symbolise 'New Nairm' or Melbourne and acknowledges the original 'Federation' of the Kulin Nation. Look for the nine 'visions' inscribed as poetic texts in the cobbles. Number 1 'Maker's Vision' describes Bunjil's creation of the Kulin people and the Yarra River. A flyer is available from the Visitors Centre. Artist: Paul Carter. **Location**: Federation Square, Flinders Street. Melway: 1B P10.

B. Indigenous art collection, Ian Potter Centre: National Gallery of Victoria (NGV), Federation Square

Federation Square is home to the world's largest Aboriginal and Torres Strait Islander art collection, based at the Ian Potter Centre, National Gallery of Victoria, with free access to the public galleries (see Site 2, p. 12). **Location:** Federation Square, Flinders Street. Melway: 1B Q10.

Right: Texts inscribed into the Federation Square Plaza include *Maker's Vision* describing the creation of the Melbourne area or 'Nearamnew' by Bunjil.

Top: Carved wooden sculpture, *Birrarung Willam* installation. Top right: Metal shields representing the five groups of the Kulin nation. Above: Rock engraving, *Birrarung Willam* installation. Photographs by Hari Ho.

C. Birrarung Marr Park

Birrarung Marr Park on the river and adjacent to Federation Square is home to two large installations. Birrarung Willam (River Camp) is a grassy area surrounded by rocks marking the famous Yarra Bank speakers' corner where Aboriginal civil rights leaders once debated with crowds. The area includes a performance space and metal shields representing five groups of the Kulin nation. Oral history stories can be heard on the Art Play wall — increase or decrease the volume level by touching the wall. Artists: Vicki Couzens, Lee Darroch, and Treahna Hamm.

The second installation, *Eel Trap* is a winding sculpture celebrating the Yarra River and the culture and knowledge associated with the annual hunting and trapping season of eels. Artists: Fiona Clarke and Ken McKean. **Location:** Birrarung Marr. Melway: 2F H6, J6.

D. William Barak Bridge

William Barak Bridge is a 525-metre pedestrian walkway that links Federation Square and Birrarung Marr to the Yarra Park sporting precinct. It opened in time for the 2006 Commonwealth Games. Barak was a famous Wurundjeri Ngurungaeta and artist (see pp. ii, 83 & 87).

There are spectacular views from its span as well as a sound installation, *Proximities*, by David Chesworth and Sonia Leber. It includes a welcome song in Woiwurrung by Wurundjeri Elder Joy Murphy Wandin. Design: Cox Architects and Planners. **Location:** Federation Square, Flinders Street and Batman Avenue. Melway: 2F K6.

E. River Yarra (Rainbow) Pedestrian Bridge

The pedestrian bridge to Southgate is known locally as the Rainbow Bridge. Binbeal the rainbow was the son of the ancestral hero Bunjil who created the river in the Dreaming. A canal enters the river twenty metres east of the bridge below the rail subway entrance. This was the junction where a creek (now under Elizabeth Street) met the river. The Kulin believed that spirit children awaited their rebirth at the junction of such waterways. A stairway on the bridge descends to a cafe surrounded by the waters of the Yarra. **Location:** Connecting Northbank to Southbank Promenade, Yarra River. Melway: 2F F6.

Top: William Barak Bridge. Above: River Yarra (Rainbow) Pedestrian Bridge.

Gayip, artists Nadim Karam and Mandy Nicholson.

F. *Gayip* and *The Travellers*

The *Gayip* sculpture in Queensbridge Square on Southbank symbolises Victoria's Kulin clans which met regularly in this location before settlement for marriage, trading, dispute resolution, ceremonies, dance and storytelling. It is the first of the sculptures of *The Travellers*, which is an extraordinary multicultural installation on historic Sandridge Bridge where 128 glass screens record both the Koorie and immigrant history of Victoria. *The Travellers* consists of ten giant steel sculptures, nine of which are fixed to a bogie system and 'travel' across Sandridge Bridge symbolising nine eras of immigration. *Gayip* is the only sculpture fixed to land, symbolising the unique status of Australia's first inhabitants. Artists: Nadim Karam and Mandy Nicholson.

Gayip (Gaggip) was an Aboriginal ceremony that strengthened bonds of unity. In 1843, 300 people from the Woiwurrung, Boon Wurrung and Taungurong clans gathered on the Yarra River at its junction with Merri Creek for the summer solstice and performed seven dances over nine days. The final dance brought all the parties into the centre of the camp and proclaimed goodwill to all. They explained to Assistant Protector William Thomas, 'when one tribe has Gaggip with another, from that time they are friends'. **Location:** Sandridge Bridge and Queensbridge Square, Southbank. Melway: 2F D7.

G. *Scar: A Stolen Vision*

This Aboriginal art installation was created in 2001 and moved to the riverbank at Enterprize Park where the town of Melbourne was founded by British settlers who disembarked from the schooner *Enterprize* in 1835. Seven Koorie artists from across Victoria have inscribed their stories on thirty recycled pier poles evoking personal interpretations of their culture, history and spiritual beliefs and reflecting reconciliation issues. The project was conceived by Kimba Thompson of Sista Girl Productions inspired by traditional 'scarred trees' made when cutting bark for shields, shelter, containers and canoes from trees.

Artists: Karen Casey, Ray Thomas, Maree Clarke, Glenn Romanis, Craig Charles, Ricardo Idagi and Treahna Hamm. **Location:** Enterprize Park, Flinders Street, Northbank, Yarra River, Melbourne. Melway: 2F C7.

Scar: A Stolen Vision, Aboriginal art installation. Seven Koorie artists have inscribed their stories on thirty recycled pier poles. Photographs by Hari Ho.

H. The Tribute Garden

The steps to the multicultural Tribute Garden in the rear courtyard of the Immigration Museum are etched with the names of all the Kulin clans of Victoria. Artist: Evangelos Sakaris. **Location:** Immigration Museum, 400 Flinders Street, Melbourne. Melway: 2F C6, D6.

The steps to the Tribute Garden.

Bunjil, artist Bruce Armstrong.

Webb (Eel trap) Bridge, artist Robert Owen, architects, Denton Corker Marshall.

I. Webb (Eel Trap) Bridge

Webb Bridge, locally known as Eel Trap Bridge, is a pedestrian and cycling bridge in the extraordinary design of a Koorie eel trap. It links new residences of Yarra Edge on the south side of the Yarra to the venues of Melbourne Docklands on the north side. Design: Architects Denton Corker Marshall and artist Robert Owen. **Location:** near South Wharf Promenade, Docklands, west of the Polly Woodside Tall Ship. Melway: 2E G9.

J. *Bunjil*

This 25-metre, 20-tonne sculpture towers over the southern entry to the Docklands on Wurundjeri Way. It was inspired by Bunjil the wedge-tailed eagle, spirit creator of the Kulin nation. Unveiled in 2002, it has become one of the Dockland's most well-known landmarks. Plans are being made to eventually move it to a nearby location. Artist: Bruce Armstrong. **Location:** Wurundjeri Way, Docklands. Melway: 2E K7.

The site of Queens Bridge, *Melbourne from the falls*, Eliezer Levi Montefiore, 1866. State Library of Victoria, H3831. Right: Queens Bridge, site of the former Yarra Yarra Falls.

Yarra Yarra Falls

Queens Bridge on the Yarra River is built on the basalt rocks of the former Yarra Yarra Falls, a central rendezvous point for clans of the Kulin nation who met here at least twice a year for law, social and ceremonial purposes. The waterfall provided access to plentiful fresh water by separating the salty downstream water from the freshwater above. The Kulin were also able access to both sides of the river by using the rocks as stepping stones.

The Yarra River is the defining landscape feature of the Melbourne city centre but its naming indicates the cultural misunderstandings which often characterised interactions between the settlers and the Koories.

After settlement, a dam was built at the falls to improve the water supply, but it contributed to disastrous floods in the early years of settlement. The waterfall was blown up with explosives in 1860 as it prevented larger ships going further upstream.

Location: Queens Bridge connects Queensbridge Square on Southbank to the north bank of the Yarra River near the Immigration Museum. Melway: 2F C6 D7. The site is a ten minute walk from either Flinders or Southern Cross train stations. Queens Bridge can be reached by Melbourne City Tourist Shuttle (bus) or the free City Circle Tram which runs every ten minutes in both directions and also by tram routes 70 and 75.

The Kulin name for the Yarra River was **Birrarung** (ever flowing) but John Wedge, the surveyor with John Batman's party, named it in error as he later admitted:
On arriving in sight of the river, the two natives who were with me, pointing to the river, called out, 'Yarra Yarra', which at the time I imagined to be its name; but I afterwards learnt that the words were what they used to designate a waterfall.

Birrarung (Yarra River)

'… my grandmother and others of course would be able to have any supply of food and be able to use the reeds around the river to make all their containers, their baskets and their bowls and all those sorts of utensils. … It was a ceremonial place, ceremonies seemed to have always taken place by the river. … It was a meeting place, and when tribes wanted to cross the river that was like the boundaries, so they had to get permission to literally cross the river.'

Joy Wandin Murphy
Wurundjeri

DESCRIPTION

The world's largest collection of Aboriginal and Torres Strait Islander art is housed at the Indigenous Galleries at the Ian Potter Centre, National Gallery of Victoria, Federation Square.

LOCATION

Federation Square is opposite Flinders Street Station, opposite St Pauls Cathedral. Melway: 2F G5–6.

GETTING THERE

Public transport: Trams run frequently past the square on St Kilda Road and Swanston Street. Alight at the Flinders Street stop.

Car parking: Available at the Federation Square Car Park. Enter at the corner of Flinders and Russell Streets, or from Batman Avenue.

HOURS

10am–5pm, Tuesday to Sunday. Closed Mondays. Open all public holidays except Christmas Day & Good Friday. Open from 1pm on ANZAC Day.

The Ian Potter Centre, National Gallery of Victoria. Photograph courtesy NGV Photographic Services.

SITE 2
Indigenous art collection

The world's largest collection of Aboriginal and Torres Strait Islander art is housed at the Ian Potter Centre, National Gallery of Victoria at Federation Square.

Australian Indigenous art is the oldest continuing tradition of art in the world. Initial forms of artistic Aboriginal expression were rock carvings, body painting and ground designs, which date back more than 30,000 years. The quality and variety of the art produced is recognised throughout Australia and the world for its strength and vitality deriving from traditions that emphasised the continuous links between art, place, spirituality and storytelling. Introduced media such as paint, printmaking, fabric printing, ceramics and glassware now complement traditional arts and crafts.

A piece from the Ian Potter Centre collection; Tommy McRae, Kwatkwat c. 1835–1901, *Ceremony: Hunting Possum* c. 1880, pen and black-brown ink, red ink wash on paper, 27.6x35.8cm, National Gallery of Victoria, Af100116.

The exhibition demonstrates the physical, spiritual and ecological importance of the four elements of nature to Aboriginal people. It is devoted to describing the Dreaming associations and ancestral narratives related to fire, water, earth and wind.

The collection represents most of Australia's major historical and contemporary movements. Works include different media by a wide selection of artists including William Barak, Judy Watson, Emily Kngwarray, Uta Uta Tjangala, Albert Namatjira, Clifford Possum, Tjapaltjarri, Rover Thomas, Lin Onus and Yannima Tommy Watson. Important works from formative periods are displayed such as the Hermannsburg School, Utopia community, Papunya Collection and Warlukurlangu.

FACILITIES

Cafes, gift shop, disability access. Many venues are co-located on Federation Square including the visitors centre, restaurants, a public events space and the Australian Centre for the Moving Image. The visitors centre recommends Melbourne outlets where ethically produced Indigenous art can be purchased.

ADMISSION

Admission to the permanent collection is free. Free daily tours of the Aboriginal galleries (except Monday) are available.

TIME 1 hour.

ACTIVITIES

Birrarung Marr Park on the north bank of the Yarra River with two large Indigenous installations is nearby. The second National Gallery of Victoria (NGV International) is located ten minutes walk south at 180 St Kilda Road.

FURTHER INFORMATION

Tel: (03) 8620 2222 (10am–5pm).
Web: www.ngv.vic.gov.au/visit/two-locations

Koorie Heritage Trust exhibition. Photograph by Steven Rhall, courtesy Koorie Heritage Trust.

SITE 3
Koorie Heritage Trust

Gnokan Danna Murra Kor-Ki (Give me your hand my friend) — Motto of the Trust

The Koorie Heritage Trust was established to 1985 by Koorie leader Jim Berg with support from prominent human rights and Indigenous rights lawyers Ron Castan QC and Ron Merkel QC, to promote awareness of Koorie culture and to provide a means for Aboriginal control and preservation of important heritage material. The Trust's building operates exhibition spaces, a gallery, museum, library, gift shop, education programs, an oral history program and a genealogy service to connect Koorie people with their family and country.

Exhibitions are housed in three stunning galleries in a purpose-built cultural centre. The Darren Pattie-Bux Gallery and Gandel Family Foyer Gallery are located on the ground floor and display important work from both established and emerging Koorie artists. The Aunty Joyce Johnson Gallery, on the first floor, features established Koorie artists,

Koorie Heritage Trust education program. Photograph by Steven Rhall, courtesy Koorie Heritage Trust.

in-coming travelling exhibitions and displays from the Trust. The building houses one of the largest Indigenous collections in the country including 10,000 weavings, baskets, eel traps, paintings and other artefacts. The gift shop is a popular outlet for an extensive range of books as well as artefacts by Koorie artists from Victoria and other parts of Aboriginal Australia. The Trust can link visitors to important local artists and works to bridge the cultural gap between Koories and wider communities.

At the time of publication the Trust was in the process of moving to larger premises in the city centre. Please check their location before you visit.

Right Jim Berg, *Fishing spear,* 2009. Photograph by Steven Rhall, courtesy Koorie Heritage Trust.

THE THREE MOOGJIS

'These three men came together to fight and do what was right and to right what was wrong.' — *Power and the Passion: Our Ancestors Return Home*, 2010.

In the 1970s, Ron Castan QC, Ron Merkel QC, and Jim Berg became close colleagues and a formidable force in Victoria for Aboriginal restorative justice. They worked closely together in the Victorian Aboriginal Legal Service on numerous cases and in 1985 founded the Koorie Heritage Trust Inc. Their personal bond in a common cause earned them the title of The Three Moogjis. This phrase could be loosely translated as The Three Amigos.

The Moogjis first met in a small office in Fitzroy in 1972 when 'the two Ronnies' hired Jim Berg as a field officer for the new Victorian Aboriginal Legal Service. Berg soon became executive officer and by the mid-1970s, he had arranged for the service to become a fully self-managed Aboriginal organisation. Castan and Merkel continued to provide legal advice and representation on request.

The catalyst for creating the Trust occurred in the early 1980s after Berg was appointed as an inspector for the *Victorian Archaeological and Aboriginal Relics Preservation Act 1972*. He soon exercised his role by impounding a collection of Aboriginal artefacts being auctioned in Melbourne. However the Supreme Court upheld an appeal by the auction house in 1984.

As Ron Merkel wrote, 'Although Jim lost the battle with Joel's he won the war'. The extensive publicity alerted Aboriginal communities, the public and businesses of the important issues at stake. Only three months later, the new *Commonwealth Aboriginal and Torres Strait Islander Heritage Protection Act 1984* strengthened the powers of Aboriginal communities to control cultural material. Inspired by Jim Berg's example, the NSW Aboriginal Land Council launched a similar action against auction house Sotheby's.

These events revealed the urgent need to purchase precious items being auctioned for sale to save Aboriginal cultural heritage from disappearing into private collections and overseas. The two Ronnies helped raise the urgently needed funds. The Koorie Heritage Trust was created to manage the rescued objects and to acquire other important cultural artefacts on behalf of Koorie communities in southeast Australia. The Trust has continued to grow, earning the support of state and federal governments and many others.

In 1999, The Moogji Lounge in the Trust building was named in honour of Ron Castan who died suddenly at the age of 59 following surgery. He is also remembered by the Castan Centre for Human Rights Law at Monash University.

After his death, Senator Aden Ridgeway famously described this quietly spoken Moogji as 'the great white warrior against racism'. His battles for Indigenous justice in Australia included the Gove land rights case *Milirrpum v Nabalco Pty Ltd (1971)*, *Koowarta v Bjelke-Petersen (1982)* and *Wik Peoples v Queensland (1996)*. He spent ten years as counsel assisting Eddie Mabo fight 'the Mabo Case' — *Mabo v Queensland (No.2) (1992)* — which succeeded in recognising Aboriginal land rights for the first time and abolishing the doctrine of terra nullius.

Left: *The first execution*, WFE Liardet 1842. State Library of Victoria, H28250/14. Above: Bowen Terrace, corner of Franklin and Bowen Streets.

SITE 4
Freedom fighters execution site

The view from the corner of Bowen Street and Franklin Street (Bowen Terrace) is of the peaceful life of academia on the RMIT University City Campus. It is hard to reconcile it with the brutal scenes recorded of Victoria's first execution near this site on the 20 January 1842.

Five Aboriginal people from Tasmania were tried for the murder of two whalers after a series of raids on settlers south of Melbourne. The two men were called Maulboyheenner and Tunnerminnerwait (Jack Napoleon). The three women were Truganini, Planobeena (Fanny) and Pyterruner (Matilda) (see p. 19).

Over 5000 people attended the execution of the two convicted men at 'Gallows Hill' in a bizarre carnival-like atmosphere. Some spectators jumped onto the coffins to get a better view. From a distance, Koories grimly witnessed British justice at work. The three women were deported back to Flinders Island.

Jan Roberts describes the events in her book, *Jack of Cape Grim* (see Reference list, p. 138). In 1839, the five accused had been brought by Chief Protector George Robinson to Port Phillip from Flinders Island to assist him in mediation with Melbourne's Kulin. They were all survivors of the notorious Black Wars in Tasmania. The three women had previously

Right: Maulboyheenner (top) and Tunnerminnerwait were hanged on 20 January 1842. Courtesy the British Museum.

17

CITY CENTRE & SURROUNDS

DESCRIPTION

In 1842, the execution of two Aboriginal freedom fighters took place at Gallows Hill. An annual commemoration service is held at Bowen Terrace on 20 January to acknowledge past injustices.

LOCATION

Bowen Street is the pedestrian thoroughfare through RMIT University in La Trobe Street. The area is between Building 9 and 12. The Ngarara Willim Centre for Aboriginal and Torres Strait Islander students is in Building 12. Melway: 2B E12.

GETTING THERE

Frequent trams travel along Swanston Street; there is the free city circle tram and via Melbourne Central train station.

FACILITIES

A public cafe and courtyard is in the RMIT Francis Ormond Building (open 7am–5pm). Historic Storey Hall houses the public art and design RMIT Gallery. Accessible toilets. RMIT city campus is adjacent to the State Library of Victoria, Melbourne City Baths, Chinatown and the Greek Precinct.

TIME 20 minutes.

suffered abuse from whale hunters and Tunnerminnerwait survived a massacre of his tribe in 1828. Their guerrilla war started in late 1841, immediately after Tunnerminnerwait returned from a journey assisting Robinson collecting testimony about massacres in the Western District of Victoria.

William J Thomas, the Assistant Protector's son, suggested Tunnerminnerwait's motives: *'There was a man among them, a man superior in every respect to the others, he had been a leading man, a chief in his own country and he was the leader of the malcontents here — his name was Napoleon. He talked about how they had suffered at the hands of the white man, how many of their tribe had been slain, how they had been hunted down in Tasmania — now was the time for revenge...'*

The accused were forbidden to give evidence in their defence or to call Aboriginal witnesses because they were deemed unable to take the Christian oath. Their young lawyer, Redmond Barry, challenged whether British courts had jurisdiction over Aboriginal people. The jury recommended leniency 'on account of general good character and the peculiar circumstances in which they are placed'. However, the government was determined to deter other acts of rebellion.

The executed men were buried at the Old Melbourne Cemetery, the site of today's Queen Victoria Market (see Site 5, p. 20) .

Since 2006, public commemorations have been held every 20 January at Bowen Terrace to acknowledge injustices of the past and to highlight the unfinished business that still exists between Aboriginal and non-Aboriginal Australians.

In December 2013 the Melbourne City Council voted unanimously to establish a permanent memorial marking the events of 1842.

Trugernana, Beattie photograph of Thomas Bock watercolour c.1840. Reproduced with permission from the Tasmanian Museum & Art Gallery, Q13009.

TRUGANINI IN MELBOURNE

Truganini is a famous Aboriginal Tasmanian but her activities in Melbourne are less known.

She was the daughter of a clan leader during the violent Black Wars in Tasmania in 1828–32. Most of her family had been murdered or abducted by the time she met Protector George Robinson at the age of 17. She and her husband Woorraddy acted as cultural intermediaries for Robinson in his successful campaign to persuade Aboriginal people to lay down their arms peacefully in return for safe passage to Flinders Island (in Bass Strait near Tasmania). Robinson was richly rewarded by the government. However, the Aboriginal death rates on Flinders Island were devastating, partly due to Robinson's neglect.

Robinson used his 'successes' to convince the British government to appoint him Chief Protector in the new district of Port Phillip.

In 1839, he brought Truganini, Woorraddy and fourteen others from Flinders Island to Melbourne to assist him but he eventually lost interest in them. Left to their own devices, Truganini and four others decided to foment an uprising against white occupation in the districts south of Melbourne. During her capture she apparently survived a gunshot wound to the head. In 1842, she was deported with two other female rebels, Planobeena (Fanny) and Pyterruner (Matilda), back to Flinders Island. Her husband died during the voyage. In her later years she lived in Oyster Cove, Tasmania, near Bruny Island, her birthplace.

By 1869, few of her community remained alive. Before Truganini's death in 1876, she requested that her ashes be scattered at sea close to her birth place. Instead her skeleton was exhumed and displayed in Tasmania until 1947 and exhibited in Melbourne in 1888 and 1904. From 1965 however increasing concern was expressed by the public, church authorities, media and Aboriginal groups that Truganini's original wishes should be honoured. By April 1976 the Tasmanian government had legislated to provide for cremation of the skeleton. Aboriginal community members from Warnambool in Victoria, who claimed descent from Truganni, initially opposed the cremation in preference for burial. Vivienne Rae Ellis has described the intense controversy in *Trucanini: Queen or Traitor*. Finally in April 1976, Truganini's remains were cremated and scattered according to her wishes in D'Entrecasteaux Channel.

Truganini led an extraordinary life in extraordinary times. Small in stature, she showed the defiance, courage and character to make her own choices in a society that destroyed her community. The information she gave to Robinson which he recorded in his journals is a priceless ethnographic record of Tasmanian Aboriginal culture.

SITE 5
Old Melbourne Cemetery site

Queen Victoria Market attracts crowds of shoppers every year and is one of Melbourne's most popular tourist destinations. However, few are aware that Melbourne's largest market is built over the graves of an estimated 9000 of Melbourne's early settlers as well as Koories, located under the car park and adjacent sheds.

The first eight or so people to die in Melbourne were buried in nearby Flagstaff Hill in 1836. One year later the Old Melbourne Cemetery opened on the site of today's Queen Victoria Market. It was filled within a short period, although burials in family-owned plots continued until 1917.

In 1924, despite public protests, the cemetery land was resumed by the state government for the market. Only 914 bodies were exhumed from 10,000 graves and re-interred, mainly in the Old Pioneers section of Fawkner Memorial Park. The remaining 9000 graves are easily disturbed by building works. The only remaining grave monument is that of settler John Batman who initiated the Melbourne Treaty in 1835.

On the 7 and 12 November 1990, two unknown graves were unearthed during building of a shed on the site of the former Aboriginal burial section. An autopsy, funded by the Melbourne City Council, found that the bodies were of young adult men, 20 to 30 years of age. The first man was of mixed Aboriginal and European descent. He was short (162 cm) and very heavily built. He had smoked a clay pipe. The second man was shorter (152cm), very fine boned, and of mixed Aboriginal and Asian descent. Both men may have carried out heavy manual work. The remains were respectfully removed for traditional Return to Country rites and burial.

Aboriginal freedom fighters Tunnerminnerwait and Maulboyheenner were buried outside the cemetery wall after their execution in 1842.

The memorial to John Batman. An apology to Melbourne's Koories has been recently added to the memorial.

The Koorie Heritage Trust and other community groups are keen to ensure the remaining graves are respected and undisturbed by future development.

Car parking: Metered car parking is available in surrounding streets.

HOURS

Market trading hours are 6am–2pm, Tuesday and Thursday; 6am–5pm, Friday; 6am–3pm, Saturday; and 9am–4pm, Sunday. It is closed on public holidays.

FACILITIES

Built in 1876, the market is a colourful and popular destination offering fruit and vegetables, delicatessen supplies, clothing and cafes. 'Koorie Connections — Altair', 155 Victoria Street, sells quality Aboriginal and Torres Strait Islander art and products. Accessible toilets on Queen Street plaza.

TIME 30 minutes.

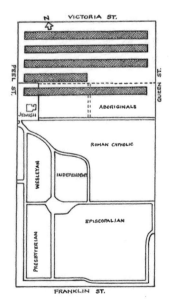

Map of the Old Melbourne Cemetery. The bars at the top represent early market stalls. Most of the remaining area is a carpark today.

DESCRIPTION

Bunjilaka Cultural Centre, Melbourne Museum, hosts permanent and temporary exhibitions, a gallery showcasing Aboriginal artists, education programs as well as gallery talks and tours.

LOCATION

The centre is located at 11 Nicholson Street, Carlton just north of the central city in the historic Carlton Gardens. Melway: 43 K5.

GETTING THERE

Public transport: Tram 86 or 96 to the corner of Nicholson and Gertrude Streets; free City Circle Tram to Victoria Parade; city loop train to Parliament Station; bus routes 250, 251 and 402 to Rathdowne Street; and free City of Melbourne Tourist Shuttle Bus to stop No. 4.

Car parking: The Melbourne Museum undercover car park is open daily from 6am–midnight. Enter via Rathdowne Street or Nicholson Street.

HOURS

Open daily 10am–5pm. Closed Good Friday and Christmas Day.

TIME 60–90 minutes.

Above and right: the Bunjilaka Cultural Centre at the Melbourne Museum. Photographs by Hari Ho.

SITE 6
Bunjilaka Cultural Centre

Bunjilaka is the Aboriginal Centre at Melbourne Museum, a venue of Museum Victoria. The name was selected after consultation with the traditional owners of Melbourne. Bunjil was a significant creation ancestor for most of Victoria's Aboriginal wurrungs and 'aka' means land or place. Together, Bunjilaka can be interpreted as 'creation place'. The centre opened in October 2000. Its purpose is to empower Aboriginal people to interpret their own cultural heritage for both Aboriginal and non-Aboriginal people.

Bunjilaka holds Aboriginal cultural heritage items from a collection that is one of the most significant in the world. It also has exhibition and performance spaces, as well as private areas such as a keeping place where the community can meet and view their cultural heritage material.

The Museum recognises the rights and perspectives of Aboriginal people and, through Bunjilaka, aims to further partnerships with Aboriginal communities, promote reconciliation to all visitors and actively support Indigenous rights and perspectives through exhibitions, performances and activities.

FACILITIES

The Museum houses a permanent collection in eight galleries, including one for children. The IMAX theatre shows films daily from 10am with discounted tickets when combined with a visit to Melbourne Museum. Guided tours are available in the Museum and to the nearby World Heritage listed Royal Exhibition Building. Accessible toilets.

ADMISSION

Adult entry is $10.00. Children (3–16) and those with concessions are free.

FURTHER INFORMATION

Tel: 13 11 02
Web: www.museumvictoria. com.au/bunjilaka/

An Aboriginal Cultural Heritage Advisory Committee comprising of twenty-two representatives from the Victorian Aboriginal communities offers advice and leadership on Indigenous issues and is another means of consultation with communities.

Bunjilaka Aboriginal Cultural Centre hosts a permanent exhibition as well as temporary exhibitions. The exhibition, *First Peoples*, takes visitors on a journey through time and place to experience stories of Aboriginal culture, identity, community and survival. More than 600 historic and contemporary artefacts are on exhibition from across Victoria and Australia.

The Birrarung Gallery showcases new and emerging artists alongside established ones, exploring the talent, stories and cultural pride of Victorian Aboriginal Art. It hosts three exhibitions a year as part of the Community Art Program which range from photography, sculpture and works on canvas to digital media and installation.

Educational programs are also offered by Bunjilaka including exhibitions, activities, workshops and programs for all levels from preschool, tertiary to adult education. Koorie community gallery talks and tours are included. Online resources are also available.

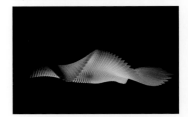

Bunjil's Wings, a kinetic sculptural and audiovisual installation that chronicles the Creation of Countries. Photograph by Hari Ho.

DESCRIPTION

Billibellary's Walk is a self-guided Indigenous interpretation trail though the historic campus of the University of Melbourne linking ten locations. The University's visual arts museum (Ian Potter Museum of Art) holds a rare collection of Indigenous art.

LOCATION

The walk starts at the University of Melbourne entrance gate three in Swanston Street between the University Information Centre and the Ian Potter Museum of Art, 800 Swanston Street. It finishes at University Square in Grattan Street, Parkville. Brochures are available with maps and information online (www.murrupbarak.unimelb.edu.au) or from Murrup Barak on campus. Melway: 2B E6–7.

GETTING THERE

The University is a ten minute walk from Melbourne's city centre.

Public transport: Trams run to the University along Swanston Walk in the city centre.

Murrup Barak, Melbourne Indigenous Development Institute (Stop 5 on Billibellary's Walk). The Institute carries out a range of activities to enhance the quality and outcome of Indigenous teaching, learning and research across the University of Melbourne. Photography by Hari Ho.

SITE 7
Billibellary's Walk

Billibellary's Walk is a self-guided Indigenous interpretation trail though the University of Melbourne. It provides a narrative for visitors to explore and imagine the University landscape across time and seasons while considering the social and cultural constructions of 'place'.

The trail was developed with support from the Wurundjeri Council and Wurundjeri elder Margaret Gardiner. The walk is named in honour of Billibellary, the highly respected Ngurungaeta of the Wurundjeri willam clan of the Woiwurrung.

The University opened in 1854 and it is one of Australia's oldest and most distinguished academic institutions. Its architecture evokes images of Eton and Cambridge. The Redmond Barry building, located on the trail, honours the former judge of the Supreme Court who founded the University. Barry arrived in Melbourne in 1837. One of his

Four River Red Gums, predating the University, represent Stop 3 on Billibellary's Walk. River Red Gums were an essential source of shelter, bark for canoes and tools for the Wurundjeri people. Photograph by Hari Ho.

HOURS

9am–5pm. The Ian Potter Centre is open 10am–5pm, Tuesday to Friday; and 12 noon–5pm, Saturday and Sunday.

ADMISSION Free.

FACILITIES

A wide variety of shops, services and cafes are found in the Student Union Building and there are many attractive gardens and quadrangles. Accessible toilets.

TIME 60–90 minutes.

FURTHER INFORMATION

Tel: 1800 457 428
Web: www.murrupbarak. unimelb.edu.au

OTHER ACTIVITIES

The Melbourne General Cemetery is a short walk north. It contains the grave and headstone of Boon Wurrung clan leader Derrimut (see Site 19 p. 70).

early court roles was as the Aboriginal Advocate. He actively defended five freedom fighters including Tunnerminnerwait and Truganini during their murder trial in 1842 (see Site 4, p. 17).

The ten locations on the trail include Murrup Barak, the University's Institute of Indigenous Development which is located in the historic Old Physics Building next to the Student Union. It houses an exhibition of Indigenous achievers. Murrup Barak was established in 2009 to initiate and promote Aboriginal programs. Its Aboriginal student centre aims to support students on campus and increase enrolments. The University has developed a Reconciliation Action Plan to promote respectful relationships between the University and Indigenous Australians and offers a number of Indigenous scholarships.

The Ian Potter Museum of Art at the start of the walk is the University's visual arts museum. The Leonhard Adam Collection contains significant Indigenous artworks including thirty-six painted barks from Groote Eylandt acquired in 1946.

BILLIBELLARY

Billibellary (c. 1799–1846) was the highly respected and influential Ngurungaeta of the Wurundjeri willam clan of the Woiwurrung.

He was an astute man and of powerful build, who worked with the British settlers to achieve the best possible outcomes for his people.

On 8 June 1835, Billibellary was one of the eight Aboriginal leaders present at the Tanderrum, or Melbourne Treaty, with John Batman's party. His name was recorded as Jaga Jaga (also spelled Jika Jika).

In 1839, Billibellary protested the breach of the treaty when the government instructed the clans to leave Melbourne. He said, 'Why you want Black Fellows away? Plenty long time ago Meregeek Batman come here. Black Fellows stop long long time.'

Billibellary's power extended to his shared custodianship of the well-known axe quarry at Mount William which was a source of prized greenstone axe heads. Clans required his permission to access the site.

Assistant Protector William Thomas greatly admired Billibellary and said Billibellary had saved his life more than once. They were very different men, one a devout Methodist and the other an initiated Kulin spokesman, yet they managed to find common cause and built a relationship of trust.

In 1840, Billibellary named his infant daughter, Susannah, in gratitude to Thomas's wife. She had nursed Simon Wonga, Billibellary's son, while he was recovering from influenza.

Billibellary's influence was demonstrated when Thomas asked him in 1842 for permission to implement the colonial plan to create a Native Police Corps. Billibellary deliberated for seven days before he agreed but he later resigned because of police actions against the Kulin. In January 1844, Thomas was in fear of his life after an altercation at a tribal gathering at Merri Creek. Billibellary allowed him to sleep in his own *miam* (shelter) for safety. Weeks later when Thomas departed for several months, he entrusted the key to the Protectorate Store to Billibellary. The Merri Creek Aboriginal School at Dights Falls in 1845 was initially supported by Billibellary but his death on 10 August 1846 from lung disease lead to a drop in numbers (see Site 14, p. 52).

Billibellary was buried close to where the Yarra River meets Merri Creek. Today a Koorie garden honours his life.

William Thomas lamented, 'It may be said of this Chief and his tribe what can scarce be said of any tribe of located parts of the colony that they never shed white man's blood nor have white men shed their blood. I have lost in this man a valuable councillor in Aboriginal affairs.'

Billibellary's son, Simon Wonga became the next clan leader. He continued his father's attempts to seek permanent land for the Kulin, eventually helping to establish Coranderrk Aboriginal Station (see p. 87).

SITE 8
Fitzroy Gardens scarred tree

Scarred trees are evidence of Aboriginal occupation both pre-contact and after European settlement. The scarred tree is located midway between two popular tourist destinations: Olga Cohn's Fairy tree and Captain Cook's Cottage. These two places, which commemorate the mythologies of Europe and the British explorer who claimed Australia, receive many thousands of visitors while few are aware of the testament to Aboriginal culture nearby.

DESCRIPTION
The base of an Aboriginal scarred tree is located in one of Melbourne's best known and oldest parks near the city centre.

LOCATION
Corner of Lansdowne Street and Wellington Parade. The tree is located beside an asphalt path, 80 metres from Wellington Parade, in the south-eastern part of the gardens. It is near Sinclair's Cottage. Melway: 2G C4.

GETTING THERE
Public transport: Alight at Parliament Station and walk to site. Alternatively, take tram number 48 or 75 from Flinders Street.

Car parking: Wellington Parade, East Melbourne.

Cycling/walking trail: The tree is a ten-minute bicycle ride from the main Yarra River Trail.

FACILITIES
Pavilion Teahouse and accessible toilets.

TIME 20 minutes.

Above: The scarred tree at Fitzroy Gardens.

'We believe it was a birthright to care for this land and it was constantly taught to you by your extended family as you grew up so as an adult you were responsible, educated person on how to survive on this land and benefit your community and Country. We were part of this Country, why wouldn't we care for it?'

Bill Nicholson
Wurundjeri

Several hundred trees in and around Melbourne show the effects of having their bark removed by the Kulin. Some of these trees have died. Others, majestic in size, are the only living witnesses of the change from a hunter–gatherer culture to an urbanised technological society. Scarred trees are important because they provide information about places of Aboriginal activity and other possible sites such as scatters of stone tools.

The size and the shape of the scars indicate the possible use of the bark. The large oval scar on the Fitzroy Gardens tree was probably made by removing bark for shelter. The Kulin word for bark and shelter and place is the same: willam.

The Wurundjeri believe that Scarred Trees which harvest resources while showing respect to the life of the tree, indicate how their ancestors managed the land sustainably for 30,000 years, or since Bunjil made humans on the banks of the Birrarung and gave them the knowledge to properly care for Country. — Griffin et. al, 2013.

Native encampment on the banks of the Yarra, watercolour with graphite pencil and glazing medium, John Cotton, c. 1842. La Trobe Library, State Library of Victoria, b28308.

SITE 9
Melbourne Cricket Ground

Yarra Park, home to the Melbourne Cricket Ground (MCG), has a rich Aboriginal history as a willam and corroboree ground.

The park contains many trees of great age. Two red gum scarred trees, surrounded by iron picket fences, have plaques which describe how their scars resulted from the removal of bark by the Kulin for canoes or other implements. These trees were once much closer to the Yarra (Birrarung) River, however, in 1899, engineers 'straightened' the river by removing two loops. The northern loop is now Gosch's Paddock adjacent to Yarra Park. The southern loop is now a pond in the Royal Botanic Gardens.

Settler William Kyle arrived in Melbourne on 2 October 1841 at the age of nine. He later recalled:

> At the time of our arrival in Melbourne there was a fairly large black population. The yarra yarra tribe camped on the land now occupied by the Melbourne and Richmond cricket ground where they held numerous Corroborees of much interest to the white people. In flood time

DESCRIPTION

Yarra Park, home of the MCG, is a former Aboriginal willam and corroboree area. Two scarred 'canoe' trees are located in the park. It contained the former Police Paddock and Barracks where the Native Police Corps were stationed. The MCG is the 'home of football', an early form of which was played by Aboriginal people known as Marngrook.

Top left: Aerial view of the MCG. Photograph by Peter Dunphy, Tourism Victoria. Above: Scarred 'canoe' tree, MCG park.

Scarred tree, Yarra Park, east of Gate 4 of the MCG.

LOCATION

The two scarred trees are located in Yarra Park uphill from the MCG. One is 100 metres uphill (east) from Gate Four. The second is a further 100 metres uphill. The Police Barracks housing the Native Police were on the corner of Hoddle Street and Wellington Parade. Melway: 2G E6.

GETTING THERE

Public transport: Tram numbers 75, 48, and 70 from the City. Bus 246 stops in Punt Road.

Car parking: Available in nearby streets.

Cycling/Walking: The main Yarra River Trail is nearby along the river.

FACILITIES

Accessible public toilets near Gate Four.

TIME 30 minutes.

OTHER ACTIVITIES

The National Sports Museum at the MCG is open 10am–5pm daily, with varied access depending on sporting events. Tours of the MCG also run regularly. The William Barak pedestrian bridge links Yarra Park with Birrarung Marr and Federation Square.

they used canoes made from the bark of gum or red gum or stringy bark trees those with a curved bole for preference. These sheets from 10–16 feet long and from 2–4 feet wide, would be cut off with a stone tomahawk.

In 1841, Yarra Park was part of the Police Paddocks Reserve. The Native Police stayed at the Mounted Police Barracks on the corner of today's Punt Road and Wellington Street when they were away from their station at Nerre Nerre Warren on the Dandenong flats. In the 1840s, Mrs Charles Perry, wife of the Bishop of Melbourne lived nearby and wrote that she often saw the Native Police drilling on horseback.

In 1853, when ten acres were set aside for the use of the Melbourne Cricket Club, the Police Paddock was still full of wattle and heath and the Kulin were camping nearby.

The first game of the modern sport of Australian Rules Football is claimed to have been played at Yarra Park, near the MCG, in 1858. Both Aboriginal men and women played a form of football prior to European settlement. As early as 1839, Assistant Protector William Thomas described the popular game called *Marngrook*:

Domestic occupations of the summer season on the Lower Murray River. Composition by Mützel based on Krefft and/or Blandowski sketches and written accounts. Reproduced with permission from the Haddon Library, University of Cambridge.

The men and boys joyfully assemble when this game is to be played. One makes a ball of possum skin, somewhat elastic, but firm and strong....The players of this game do not throw the ball as a white man might do, but drop it and at the same time kicks it with his foot, using the instep for that purpose....The tallest men have the best chances in this game....Some of them will leap as high as five feet from the ground to catch the ball. The person who secures the ball kicks it....This continues for hours and the natives never seem to tire of the exercise.

Women also played Marngrook by throwing the ball high instead of kicking. In 1889, explorer, naturalist and pioneer authority on Aboriginal culture and social organisation, Alfred Howitt, recorded that the game was likely known to most tribes of south-eastern Australia and was played on a totemic basis between large groups. In Melbourne the bunjil (eagle) and waa (crow) moities of the clans played on opposite sides. The *mangurt* (ball) could be sent as a symbolic token of friendship from one tribe to another.

Left: Street art stencil of the iconic image of Nicky Winmar, Blenders Lane, Melbourne.
Right: AFL legends (from left) Glenn James, Syd Jackson and Michael Long at the launch of
Sean Gorman's book *Legends*, published by Aboriginal Studies Press, 2011.

FOOTY HEROES

The Australian Football League (AFL) celebrates the game Marngrook every year when the Sydney Swans and Essendon compete for the Marngrook Trophy.

Another event, Dreamtime at the G, celebrates the contribution of Indigenous players to the AFL. Since 2005, the match is held every May between Richmond and Essendon. These clubs were chosen because their combined team colours are the same as the colours of the Aboriginal flag.

The match is preceded by 'The Long Walk' to promote reconciliation led by former player Michael Long. It starts at Federation Square and ends at the MCG. Long is one of the most well-known and respected figures in AFL. He was a member of two premiership sides and the winner of the 1993 Norm Smith Medal. In 1995, following an on-field incident, he made a strong stand against racial abuse in the AFL, asserting that racism had no place in sport. The Long Walk is a charity inspired by his historic 650-kilometre trek to Canberra in November

2004 to get the lives of Aboriginal people back on the national agenda. Long was joined on the road by supporters from all over Australia.

Nicky Winmar, another legendary player, was named in St Kilda's Team of the Century in 2003. Both Winmar and Long were nominated as members of the AFL's Indigenous Team of the Century in 2005. Winmar was racially abused by some in the crowd while playing for St Kilda against Collingwood in 1993. When the siren sounded, an undermanned St Kilda had recorded its first win at the ground in almost two decades. Winmar spontaneously raised his guernsey, pointed to his skin and declared to his abusers, 'I'm black. And I'm proud to be black!'

The actions of both Winmar and Long are credited as catalysts for the movement against racism in Australian Rules Football. Since 1993 the AFL has implemented anti-racial and religious vilification programs and become a strong proponent for tolerance and inclusion in sport. Its school program targets more than 30,000 children every year from multicultural backgrounds to participate in Australia's game.

SITE 10
Kings Domain Resting Place

In 1985, skeletal remains of thirty-eight Victorian Koories were reburied in Kings Domain after being held for many years in the Museum of Victoria. A procession of two hundred Aboriginal people respectfully carried the remains in bark wrappings from the Museum in Carlton through the centre of the city to a burial place in parkland opposite the Queen Victoria statue.

These remains were returned to Aboriginal custody following actions taken by the Koorie Heritage Trust and other Aboriginal organisations. In 1984, Jim Berg, Director of the Victorian Aboriginal Legal Service (VALS) took action under the *Victorian Archaeological and Aboriginal Relics Preservation Act 1972* to prevent the Museum of Victoria from sending the well-known Keilor and Green Gully skulls to an international exhibition in London. VALS then learned that the University of Melbourne was in possession of the remains of 800 Aboriginal people unearthed from the Murray River by George Murray Black in the 1940s and acquired for research. VALS obtained a Supreme Court injunction to ensure the

DESCRIPTION

A granite boulder with memorial plaque and an art installation signify the sacred resting place of the remains of thirty-eight Aboriginal people from Victoria.

LOCATION

The site is located on a grassy incline in Kings Domain Avenue, eighty metres from the corner of Linlithgow Avenue and St Kilda Road on the south side of Linlithgow Avenue.Melway: 2F J8.

Left: The plaque on the resting place reads: 'Rise from this grave, release your anger and pain, as you soar with the winds, back to your homelands, there find peace with our spiritual mother the land, before drifting off into the Dreamtime.'

SITE 10

CITY CENTRE & SURROUNDS

GETTING THERE

Public transport: There are regular trams along St Kilda Road and Swanston Street.

Car parking: Metered parking is available along St Kilda Road.

Cycling/walking: There is a trail from Flinders Street Station along St Kilda Road to Kings Domain.

TIME 30 minutes.

OTHER ACTIVITIES

The memorial is a short walk from the Royal Botanic Gardens where there is an Aboriginal Heritage Walk and the site of the first mission station and reserve. It is also close by the Shrine of Remembrance. Alternatively it is a short walk to the National Gallery of Victoria, Southbank, and Federation Square.

The Dja Dja Wurrung people celebrate the repatriation of the Jaara Baby, a child who died at some stage during the 1840s to 1860s. The child's remains were discovered in 1904, and kept in storage by Museum Victoria for ninety-nine years, until in 2003 they were repatriated to the Dja Dja Wurrung community. The remains were found traditionally wrapped in possum skins along with about 130 other artifacts of both European and Aboriginal origin. Photograph by Jason Edwards, National Geographic Creative.

material was lodged at the Museum Victoria in compliance with the legislation. The remains were eventually returned to Koorie communities for reburial. This story is detailed in the book, *Power and the Passion: Our Ancestors Return Home*, by Jim Berg and Shannon Faulkhead (see Reference list, p. 138).

Since European settlement, thousands of Aboriginal remains have been removed without permission of their families or communities by collectors who often viewed them as 'rare or curious specimens'. In many cases they fetched high prices from British scientists and were shipped overseas. In 1983 Australian Aboriginal remains were still held by 180 collecting institutions in an estimated 26 countries.

Under the provisions of the *Aboriginal Heritage Act 2006* (Vic), Museum Victoria is the official repository of Aboriginal ancestral remains in the temporary custody of the state. The Museum has repatriation policies and procedures that recognise the profound contemporary cultural and spiritual significance of ancestral remains. Since 1985 the Museum has worked in partnership with Aboriginal communities to ensure the return of more than 1000 remains to traditional owner groups.

Aboriginal communities nationwide continue to actively seek the return of thousands of Aboriginal remains held by European institutions.

The ornamental lake at the Botanic Gardens. Photograph by Mark Chew, Tourism Victoria.

SITE 11
Royal Botanic Gardens

Aboriginal reserve site

Melbourne's magnificent Royal Botanic Gardens (RBG) occupies the site which the Kulin know as Tromgin.

Up to 500 members of four Kulin clans gathered at Tromgin on 28 March 1939 to greet the newly arrived Chief Protector of Aborigines, George Robinson. The colonial government recognised Tromgin was an important willam in Melbourne when it allocated the area for the first Aboriginal reserve and mission station in Melbourne. An 895-acre reserve with a permanent village and school was established to prevent the destructive conflicts that had occurred with Aboriginal people of Tasmania in the 1820s. Captain Lonsdale, Police Magistrate of Port Phillip, appointed Reverend George Langhorne to 'civilise the blacks' through education, religious instruction and farming. An Anglican mission, with three houses and a number of Aboriginal huts, was constructed in 1837.

Prominent Kulin who were associated with the mission include William Barak who attended the school and Derrimut.

DESCRIPTION

The Royal Botanic Gardens, the site known to the Kulin as Tromgin, was once an important Aboriginal camp and Melbourne's first Aboriginal reserve which included a village mission, school and later the Chief Protector's office. It also hosts a popular Aboriginal heritage walk provided by Koorie guides that explores traditional culture including the uses of plants and wildlife for food, tools and medicine.

LOCATION

Birdwood Avenue, South Yarra. Melway: 2G D12.

The plaque to Aboriginal occupation is located on the former bank of the Yarra River, five metres past the list of Directors inside Gate H, Alexandra Avenue. The lake area near the plaque is a former loop of the Yarra.

GETTING THERE

Public transport: The free Melbourne City Tourist Shuttle stops at the Gardens. Tram number 8 from Swanston Street travels along Domain Road (Gate D and Gate E).

35

Cycling/walking: Designated bicycle paths along the Yarra River and Melbourne city centre lead to the gardens from the city centre. Cycling is not allowed in the gardens.

HOURS

Daily 7.30am–sunset. The heritage walk runs Tuesday to Friday and the first Sunday of the month 11am–2.30pm. Bookings are advisable.

FACILITIES

The Gardens include the Visitor Centre at the Observatory Precinct, Ian Potter Foundation Children's Garden, Glasshouse Display, Plant Craft Cottage, visitors' shops, the Terrace Cafe and Observatory Cafe. Accessible toilets.

ADMISSION

Free. Admission fees apply for the Aboriginal heritage walk. Meet at the Visitor Centre, Observatory Gate.

TIME 1 hour.

FURTHER INFORMATION

Tel: (03) 9252 2300
Web: www.rbg.vic.gov.au

The Separation Tree, Royal Botanic Gardens, located on the path between Gate A and the Terrace Cafe.

William Buckley, the escaped convict from the early Sorrento settlement who spent thirty-two years with clans near Geelong, was employed to assist as an interpreter.

However Langhorne's plans to encourage cultivation of plots of land ignored traditional Aboriginal cultural beliefs and lifestyle. His efforts were undermined by the closeness of the settlement and there was also pressure from settlers to sell the land. Aboriginal children received rations to attend the school but eventually they all departed with their parents. Only a small number of people settled permanently at the village mission which closed in March 1839. George Robinson later administered the Port Phillip Aboriginal Protectorate from an office in the former mission from December 1839 to July 1843.

On 15 November 1851 the Native Police Corps, drawn from Melbourne's clans, was in attendance for escort duty at the Separation Tree, a 300-year-old River Red Gum near today's Terrace Cafe. Here jubilant Victorians celebrated the separation of their colony from New South Wales while the former landowners, mounted on their horses, maintained order.

Right: The Eel Bridge at the Royal Botanic Gardens. Below: *Eel hunting at Tromgin* by George Robinson, George Augustus Robinson Journals. Mitchell Library, State Library of New South Wales, A7037, vol. 16, p. 232.

HARVESTING FOOD AT TROMGIN

Eels were a staple food hunted by the Kulin. The Eel Bridge over the ornamental lake at the Royal Botanic Gardens celebrates its bountiful eel population. Chief Protector Robinson's office was beside Tromgin and in January 1841, he recorded and sketched Boon Wurrung men catching eels.

> This afternoon two native blacks of the Boongerong tribe — Niggerernaul and a lad named Dol.ler — came to my office and went to the lagoon about a quarter of a mile distant in the paddock and in a very short time caught about forty pounds of eel. I saw them catching or rather spearing them at which they are very expert. Their mode is as follows: they each had two spears called by them 1. toke.in, 2. yoke.wil.loke. The eels they call yoe.hoke. Bet Banger is father to Dol.ler.
>
> Having the two spears grasped by the right hand thus, they go in to the water and keep walking about, at the same time jabbing their spears into the mud in a sloping direction before them. If they jab in their spear which is ascertained by their feet they turn it up on the end of the spear, the second spear is jabbed into it whilst he lifts holds it down and thus kills it. If not quite dead they bite the head and throw it on shore. I bought some of the eels, twenty, and two spears made thus: half an inch stick. Wire size of that used round the rim of saucepan, it is called yoke.wil.

Aboriginal heritage walk

Established in 1846, the Royal Botanic Gardens consists of thirty-eight hectares of landscaped gardens with native and non-native vegetation including over 10,000 individual species. A popular and award-winning Aboriginal heritage walk runs regularly in the gardens.

The walk is led by Koorie guides who explore the ancestral lands of the Kulin confederacy and the traditional uses of plants for food, tools, canoes, houses and medicine. The garden wetlands, rich in plants and wildlife such as eels, turtles and waterbirds, give an insight into landscapes once common in the Melbourne area. The ninety-minute tour includes a traditional smoking ceremony and an exploration of a rich and thriving culture.

Women played a central role in the life of the clans including collecting most of the plants needed to meet the necessities of daily life. There was a social division of roles with men generally hunting larger game and women hunting smaller game, shellfish, edible roots and other plants. However, at times women did hunt larger game and men could harvest plants. The women also manufactured a large array of high quality baskets, fibre, containers and personal decorations, many of which can be seen in the Bunjilaka Centre (see Site 6, p. 22) and the Koorie Heritage Trust (see Site 3, p. 14). Women could also conduct separate ceremonial activities including corroborees.

For over thirty years Koorie communities across Victoria have collaborated with respected ethnobotanist Dr Beth Gott of Monash University to preserve information about thousands of traditional uses of plants. Her book with Nelly Zola, *Koorie Plants and Koorie People*, highlights the vast knowledge that Koories have acquired about their environment (see Reference list, p. 138).

EXAMPLES OF PLANTS COMMON TO THE MELBOURNE AREA

Top: Kabin, *Hardenbergia Violacea* (Running Postman)

The long tough stems are used for rope and the nectar is sucked from the flowers.

Middle: Karawun, *Lomandra longifolio* (Mat Rush)

The leaves are excellent for making baskets and eel traps. The base of the young leaves are eaten.

Bottom: Worike, *Banksia* sp. (Banksia)

Water is poured through the flowers to filter and sweeten it. Settlers used the stem cores of the dead flower for cleaning pipes and for candle-making.

EAST

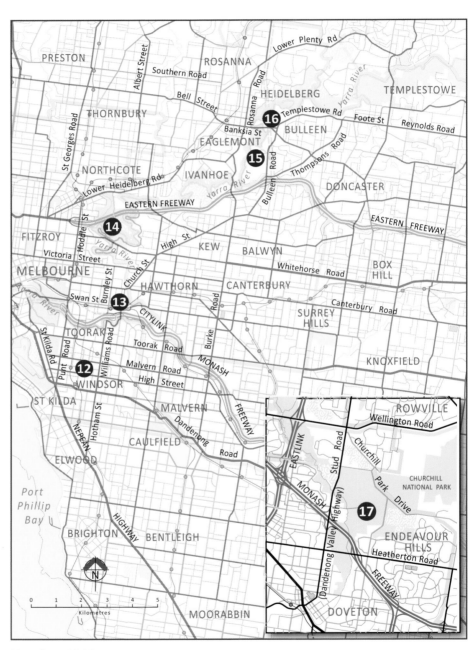

Map of sites 12–17.

EAST

As the Birrarung (Yarra River) flows from the Yarra Ranges towards Port Phillip Bay, it weaves its way through many large parks and heavily populated suburbs of Melbourne. During its course, it is joined by many smaller streams and rivers. The fertile twisting valley was the subject of many creation stories and large gatherings for the eel season at Bulleen. Most of the sites in this precinct can be found close to the Yarra River and can be easily reached by vehicle or by bicycle on the Yarra Trail.

The Yalukit willam clan of the Boon Wurrung claim the areas around the Yarra River towards the coast while the Wurundjeri clans of the Woiwurrung claim the Yarra River upriver and lands drained by its tributaries up to its source.

The first documented encounter between European explorers and the Kulin clans in Melbourne occurred in 1803 when an expedition under New South Wales Surveyor-General Charles Grimes was sent from the ship *Cumberland* to map Port Phillip. They rowed up the Yarra as far as Dights Falls where they saw Aboriginal people. The locality, today known as Yarra Bend, was one of the most popular Kulin meeting places in Victoria in the 1840s.

View towards the Eastern suburbs from the Yarra River.

SITES

12. Stonnington Indigenous history trail

13. Burnely Ngargee (corroboree) tree

    Of interest: Wurundjeri Council

14. Merri Creek Aboriginal School and the Native Police Corps and Protectorate Station

15. Bolin Bolin Billabong

16. Heide Museum, scarred tree

17. Dandenong Police Paddocks Reserve

DESCRIPTION

An Indigenous history trail with eleven interpretative markers in the City of Stonnington provides extensive information about the Aboriginal heritage of the area including clans, lifestyle, significant individuals, key locations, important events and photographs.

LOCATION

Most panels are located on or near the Yarra River particularly along Alexandra Avenue from Punt Road to Williams Road. For a guided map of the trail, the full text of the Indigenous History Markers and an Indigenous history of Stonnington visit: www.stonnington.vic.gov.au.

GETTING THERE

Car parking: Vehicle parking is available on the route.

Cycling/Walking: The Yarra River Trail is a shared bicycle and walking trail beside the river and along Alexandra Avenue that provides excellent access.

TIME 2–3 hours.

Yarra River near Como Park. Photography by Hari Ho.

SITE 12
Stonnington Indigenous History Trail

The City of Stonnington is located in Melbourne's inner east. It is home to approximately 90,000 residents living in the suburbs of Prahran, Windsor, South Yarra, Toorak, Armadale, Malvern, Malvern East, Glen Iris and Kooyong. In 2009, the city fulfilled a commitment through its Reconciliation Action Plan to acknowledge and educate the community about the traditional owners. Boon Wurrung and Wurundjeri representatives participated in the launch of the Indigenous History Trail. Eleven illustrated panels are located at important Indigenous places to provide information about historical events, places and people.

In the early days of settlement, Stonnington was a popular willam for the Melbourne clans with about eighteen meeting sites recorded. At least forty members of the Boon Wurrung people frequented Stonnington in the 1830s, including leading men of the Yalukit willam clan such as Derrimut and Ningerranaro and his sons, Bullourd, Pardeweerap and

Aboriginal camp up the Yarra, Antoine Fauchery, c. 1859. State Library of Victoria, H2476.

Mingarerer. Derrimut was well-known to residents in the neighbourhoods of Prahran and St Kilda.

The Woiwurrung, Taungurong, Wathaurong and Dja Dja Wurrung clans also gathered in Stonnington for social, ceremonial and trading purposes, arranging marriages and resolving disputes. They camped at Turruk during the 1840s, a large Aboriginal meeting ground on what is now Como Park and Thomas Oval. Today's suburb of Toorak draws its name from turruk meaning 'reedy grass.' In April 1842, Kulin clans gathered at Turruk to negotiate outstanding grievances but were forced to stop proceedings by Assistant Protector William Thomas and the Native Police, so resolutions were not reached.

The clans camped regularly along the banks of the Yarra River and Gardiners Creek which were rich in aquatic foods and wildlife. Prahran's terrain was a combination of large trees, wattle scrub and reed filled swamps. According to missionary George Langhorne, Pur-ra-ran means 'land partially surrounded by water'.

Terneet or Tivoli on Alexandra Avenue was the beautiful residence and farm of the Chief Aboriginal Protector George Augustus Robinson, where leaders of the Melbourne clans

A corroboree of the Aboriginal Australians, engraving, Calvert Samuel, 1864. National Library of Victoria, MP24/03/68/8.

'All forms of knowledge, religious and philosophical beliefs of the community were handed down to the next generation by word of mouth, by way of stories and songs and by rock, sand and bark engravings, and by dances and ceremonies.'

Wayne Atkinson
Yorta Yorta

visited and camped regularly. In fact a number of Aboriginal people were buried at Terneet.

By 1852 Assistant Protector Thomas had secured a reserve at Mordialloc for the Boon Wurrung and a reserve at Warrandyte for the Woiwurrung. The Boon Wurrung still continued to visit Stonnington at intervals, camping in Fawkner Park and sites in the western end of the municipality.

1. Hunting grounds of Chapel Street

The Yalukit willam of the Boon Wurrung had well-developed hunting equipment and techniques and an intimate knowledge of Prahran's habitats and abundant wildlife which enabled them to gain sufficient resources in about five hours per day. **Location**: Chapel St, Prahran, near Prahran Town Hall. Melway: 58 D6.

2. Meeting place for corroborees

Chapel Street was recorded as a location where numerous corroborees were observed and attended by Europeans. **Location:** Chapel St, Prahran, near Prahran Town Hall. Melway: 58 D6.

3. Home of pro-Indigenous activist Helen Baillie

Helen Baillie was a life member of the well-known Australian Aborigines' League that formed in 1936 to fight for equal rights. She opened her home in Punt Road as a hostel to Koories from across the state in the 1930–50s. **Location:** 462 Punt Road, South Yarra. Melway: 58 C2.

4. Aboriginal Village Mission

To the east of Anderson Street is the site of the Aboriginal Village Mission 1837–39 including the residence of missionary George Langhorne. It was also the site of numerous burials of Koories. **Location:** Corner of Punt Road and Alexandra Avenue. Melway: 58 C1.

Site of Melbourne's first Aboriginal mission.

5. Aboriginal campsite

During the 1830s this area was surrounded by tea-tree scrub and favoured as a frequent camping place for local clans and visiting clans from Gippsland. **Location:** Como Building, corner of Chapel Street and Toorak Road. Melway: 58 E3.

6. Melbourne's first Aboriginal mission

Missionary George Langhorne ran Melbourne's first Aboriginal reserve. It ran from 1837 to 1839 but failed by dismissing Aboriginal culture and economy. The 895-acre reserve included Tromgin, the site of the Royal Botanic Gardens. **Location:** Corner Toorak Road and Rockley Road, South Yarra. Melway: 58 F3.

7. Derrimut

Derrimut was a well-known Boon Wurrung leader who camped with his family at Tromgin (Royal Botanic Gardens), today's Melbourne High School oval and along the south bank of the Yarra River from Punt Road to the Yarra Wharf. **Location:** Yarra Trail, Alexandra Ave, South Yarra, west of Chapel Street. Melway: 58 E2.

Above: Turruk, a meeting place for Kulin clans. Right: Como Park. Photograph by Hari Ho.

8. Terneet, home of Chief Protector George Robinson

George Robinson built a grand home and estate called Terneet in 1843 where he lived until 1852. Many Koories visited and lived or were buried there. **Location**: Yarra Trail, Alexandra Ave, South Yarra, east of Chapel Street. Melway: 58 F2.

9. Lake Como, Como Park

Lake Como, Como Park to the west of Williams Road, was a favourite resort of Aboriginal people from many different clans and language groups. **Location:** Yarra Trail, Alexandra Ave, South Yarra, near Kanteen cafe. Melway: 58 G1.

10. Turruk

Turruk was a meeting place covering Como Park and Thomas Oval where up to five Kulin clans gathered for social, ceremonial and trading purposes, to arrange marriages and resolve disputes. **Location:** Yarra Trail, Alexandra Ave South Yarra at the end of Williams Road. Melway: 58 G1–2.

11. Artefacts in Kooyong Park

On 19 May 1983, the *Southern Cross* newspaper reported that about 1500 Aboriginal artefacts had been collected in Kooyong Park by a Malvern resident. The pieces of work tools and flints for cooking, engraving and hunting were thought to be over 5000 years old. **Location:** Kooyong Park, Glenferrie Road, Kooyong. Melway: 59 C3.

The Burnley Ngargee tree.

SITE 13
Burnley Ngargee (corroboree) tree

In 1926, a boy called Frederick Schrape was climbing a giant tree beside the Yarra River at Richmond when he noticed a boomerang wedged in a branch. On 18 April 1991 — sixty-five years later — his brother, Brian, formally returned it to Wurundjeri elder, Martha Nicholson, in a ceremony beside the tree in today's Burnley Park.

Sadly, the great River Red Gum has since died, but the large remaining stump is an important spiritual site for the

Wurundjeri people who believe it was a meeting place for
Kulin clans until well after European settlement as well as a
marker of clan boundaries.

When Kulin clans gathered together, dancing displays
welcomed visitors and celebrated special events. *Ngargee*
(corroborees) were witnessed in prominent sites in early
Melbourne such as the sites of today's Supreme Court, the
Melbourne Town Hall, Parliament House, South Melbourne
Town Hall, Government House, St Kilda Junction, Kooyong
Park, Victoria Park, Como Park, Fawkner Park, South Yarra,
Malvern Town Hall and Rippon Lea estate. On 21 August
1836, a corroboree was performed on Parliament Hill to
celebrate the birthday of King William IV.

Corroborees were often performed at clan gatherings
after the business of the day had finished. They were an
opportunity for celebration, to outperform other clans, to
showcase a clan's creativity in song, dance and music, and
to show appreciation to hosts or visitors. The theme of
dances was usually particular events or traditional stories.
The men painted their bodies with designs using white clay
and coloured ochres. The rhythm of the dance was often
provided by the women chanting and drumming on skins
stretched tightly between their legs. They also clapped
hands and struck sticks and boomerangs together.

Over 700 scarred trees have been reported in Melbourne.
Near the Burnley tree are many other River Red Gums which
are the most widespread eucalypt in southeast Australia.
Many have scars from human use. The Kulin used sheets of
bark from these trees to make canoes, shelters, shields and
containers. River Red Gums can live for hundreds of years,
making them a prominent feature of the landscape. These
trees often lose limbs creating large hollows which provide
important nesting sites for native wildlife such as birds and
possums.

WURUNDJERI COUNCIL

In 1985, the Wurundjeri Tribe Land and Compensation Cultural Heritage Council was established by descendants of the Wurundjeri people who, together with the Boon Wurrung, are the traditional owners of Melbourne. Members of the Council are descendants of Wurundjeri elder Bebejan, through his daughter Annie Borat (Borate) and her son Robert Wandin (Wandoon). Bebejan was a Ngurungaeta of the Wurundjeri people and a signatory on the Melbourne Treaty of 1835.

The Council works to improve the lives of Wurundjeri people and raises awareness of Wurundjeri culture and history. Welcome to Country ceremonies including speaking in language, traditional dancing and smoking rituals are also provided to the Melbourne community.

As a Registered Aboriginal Party under the *Victorian Aboriginal Heritage Act (2006)*, the council is active in managing and protecting Aboriginal cultural heritage in Wurundjeri country. In recent years the Council has taken over management of the Mount William quarry, the Sunbury earth rings, and the Coranderrk Aboriginal cemetery in Healesville (see Outer north p. 88).

In 2007, the Council opened an office at the refurbished Abbotsford Convent which provides community space for members and engages with the wider community. The site is beside the Yarra River, an important part of the creation story of the Wurundjeri with many historical places in the vicinity including Yarra Bend where the Aboriginal Protectorate, Native Police Corps and Merri Creek Aboriginal School were located (see Site 15, p. 56).

The Council is one of many organisations located at the former convent which is today a vibrant arts and cultural precinct spread over 6.8 hectares in a sweeping bend in the Yarra River. An ancient River Red Gum is located at Gate One near the Council's offices.

As history turns full circle, the Wurundjeri Council's new home is the site of the former St Heliers estate where Edward Curr (1820–89) lived with his family in 1842–50. He was a squatter who published well-known books on Aboriginal life including *Recollections of squatting in Victoria* (1883). Curr was also a member of the Aboriginal Board of Protection. He was part of a faction that was aligned with pastoralists' interests, which at times was in bitter conflict with Aboriginal people over the management of Coranderrk Aboriginal Station and other reserves (see Introduction, p. ii and Coranderrk Aboriginal Station and cemetery p. 87).

Location: 1 Heliers Street, Abbotsford. Melway: 44 G5.

Further information: Wurundjeri Council Tel: (03) 8673 0901, Email: reception@ wurundjeri.com.au

Wurundjeri Council, Abbotsford Convent.

CREATING A KOORONG

In 2012, as part of the revitalisation of Wurundjeri culture, traditional owners produced a Koorong (bark canoe) at Plenty Gorge in Wurundjeri country. The project was developed in a partnership between the Wurundjeri traditional custodians of Melbourne and surrounds as well as organisations such as Melbourne Water, Parks Victoria, Department of Sustainability and Environment, Latrobe University, and Friends of Merri Creek.

It had been a long time, perhaps generations, since the Wurundjeri had made a Koorong in Melbourne, so it was a learning process for all involved. During the reservation or mission era it was illegal to pass on Wurundjeri culture to the following generations due to government assimilation policies.

'The making of this Koorong is a significant activity; this is an example of the living culture of the Wurundjeri tribe and is part of the preservation and continuation of our cultural heritage, traditions and practices on Wurundjeri country.'

Wurundjeri Council member, Bill Nicholson

By using traditional tools and methods to build the canoe, this project aimed to increase awareness of traditional ecological knowledge and cultural practices regarding the transport and seasonal food-gathering techniques once used along the Yarra River.

The blades of the stone axes were obtained from the well-known Mount William quarry at Lancefield (see p. 84). Ochre was used to outline the Koorong shape onto a red gum tree. After cutting the outline, wooden stakes were used to carefully prise bark away from tree. The bark was then heated to shape the Koorong.

Bill Nicholson (left) and other Wurundjeri members creating a traditional Koorong or canoe using ochre, fire and stone axes from Mt William to remove bark. Photographs courtesy Coastcare Victoria.

Above: Charles Never or Murrumwiller, a pupil at the Merri Creek Aboriginal School, William Strutt, c. 1850. State Library of Victoria, H88.21/113.
Right: Site of the Merri Creek Aboriginal School.

SITE 14

Merri Creek Aboriginal School and the Native Police Corps and Protectorate Station

Merri Creek Aboriginal School

The school, also known as the Yarra Aboriginal Station or Mission, opened on 1 January 1846 near today's Dights Falls Park and was run by the Collins Street Baptist Church. Rations from the government stores were issued for the first students: twenty-six Kulin boys and girls. According to the *Port Phillip Gazette*, the wattle-and-daub school hut had, 'the Yarra in front where it curves and winds most beautifully and the Merri Creek at the back'.

There were good reasons why the school was located by Merri Creek near its junction with the Yarra River. The meeting of these two waterways form a large loop of land rich in resources called Yarra Bend which was a government reserve barred to private settlement. Its Aboriginal history is described in Ian Clark and Toby Heydon's book, *A Bend in the Yarra* (see Reference list, p. 138).

Colonial records indicate Yarra Bend was one of the greatest inter-tribal gathering places in southeast Australia. In the 1840s, Kulin clans regularly travelled hundreds of kilometres to assemble there for ceremonies, cultural matters and trade. For example, 500 Kulin assembled there in late 1842. In September 1843, a *Gageed* ceremony to expel sickness was observed at Dights Mill with 'a huge and rude temple of stringy bark covered with various hieroglyphics in chalk'. During the summer solstice almost 300 Kulin gathered to participate in the seven friendship dances of the Gayip (see Site 1, p. 8). In February 1844, 700 Kulin from eight tribes met at Merri Creek for cultural matters. In July 1847, 450 Kulin assembled there.

The neighbours of the school included the Merri Creek Protectorate Station and the Native Police Corps barracks. The nearest European neighbour was John Dight who owned the Ceres mill powered by a water race fed from the rock bar and weir. The rock falls provided the Kulin with a natural river crossing and place to trap migrating fish.

Initially, there was general support for the school and the students gave popular public performances in Melbourne demonstrating spelling, reading and singing. However, the death and burial of the esteemed Billibellary near the school in 1846 and a severe influenza epidemic in 1847 dispersed the Kulin away from the area and attendance dropped.

The school continued on with a change of teacher and a smaller number of pupils, mainly from outside Melbourne. By 1848, there were six acres of vegetables under cultivation which were sold at the Melbourne Market. In 1849, the students and teacher proudly built an ingenious cantilever bridge over the creek but they were dismayed when it was swept away in a devastating flood in 1850. With the bridge gone, their gardens and cultivated ground destroyed, and the press fanning public criticism of the school as a waste of money, the school was closed in 1851.

Right top: *Merri Creek near Dight's Falls*, Henry C Gritten, 1863. State Library of Victoria, H13203. Right bottom: Dight's Falls today.

Dights Falls Park is the site of the first known encounter in Melbourne between Europeans and the Kulin people. On 8 February 1803, Charles Grimes' survey party rowed up the Yarra to Dights Falls and saw Aboriginal people. In December 1836 John Gardiner, Joseph Hawdon and John Hepburn, the first settlers to arrive overland from Sydney, crossed Dights Falls with their cattle. They were the beginning of a new wave of land purchasers who would soon occupy the ancient lands of the traditional owners but recognised no treaty or tribute obligations.

The junction of the Yarra River and the Merri Creek near Dights Falls Park is associated with Merri Creek Aboriginal School, the Merri Creek Protectorate Station, the Koori Garden in Billibellary's memory and the Native Police Corps. It was one of southeast Australia's most popular Aboriginal meeting and trading areas in the 1840s and the site of the first Kulin encounter in Melbourne with Europeans in 1803.

LOCATION

Dights Falls Park, Trenerry Crescent, Abbotsford. Melway: 2D B6. The walking trail encircles the billabong (twenty minutes) and also connects on the far side to the Bolin Bolin Cultural Trail at the Yarra River.

GETTING THERE

From the car park on Trenerry Crescent, Abbotsford (Melway: 2D A6), a paved path leads downhill to Dights Falls on the Yarra River. Follow the path to the Merri Creek and cross the footbridge to get to the Koori Garden on your right. Turn left and walk north inland on the Merri Creek Trail for 200 metres to the former site of the Merri Creek School.

Above: Site of the Native Police Corps and Protectorate Station.

The Native Police Corps and Protectorate Station

In 1837, the colonial government set up a Native Police Corps in Port Phillip to track down insurgents, undertake law enforcement and to 'civilise' the Aboriginal men and their families. The Corps proved effective in a range of policing duties but it was also accused of excessive violence particularly in suppressing resistance by clans outside Melbourne.

The Corps headquarters was originally on the Dandenong Creek flats, known as Nerre Nerre Warren (now Narre Warren). However, in March 1842, they moved their base to Merri Creek, near Dights Falls alongside the Protectorate Station and the Merri Creek Aboriginal School because of drought. Many of their family, clan members and visitors joined them there. More than 140 men served in the Corps at some time, including most of the leaders of the Melbourne clans. A visitor, Charles Baker, described Merri Creek as a military encampment with parallel lines of fifty native shelters or 'wigwams' with Captain Henry Dana's tent at the head.

The Corps offered the opportunity to participate meaningfully in the authority of the new colony and to share the emblems of power: rank, uniforms, horses and weapons. British mounted troops are traditionally the high-ranking elite. The men showed a gift for handling horses and equipment and had their own striking uniforms. The rations and pay helped to support the men's communities. Unusually, their officers

Aboriginal troopers, Melbourne police, with English corporal, William Strutt, pencil and watercolour, 1850. Reproduced with the permission of the Victorian Parliamentary Library.

took into account the men's cultural and kinship obligations. The Corps actively recruited boys to join from the Merri Creek Aboriginal School despite objections by the Protectors. In 1845, members of eight tribes set up camp a mile from the encampment at Merri Creek, and shared the Corps' blankets and provisions. When the Assistant Protector tried to move them on, the Corps retaliated by taking over his hut.

Superintendent of Port Phillip District Charles La Trobe's plan to create a Native Police Corps proceeded only after the highly influential leader Billibellary granted permission. When he resigned, concerned about conflict of interest, many troopers followed his lead. After his death on 10 August 1846, he was buried near the junction of the Merri Creek and the Yarra River. The promontory has since been altered by floods and construction works. However, the Koori Garden, at the east end of the footbridge across the Merri Creek, honours his memory.

In September 1843 the Native Police departed Merri Creek and returned to their permanent headquarters at Nerre Nerre Werren, today the Dandenong Police Paddocks Reserve (see Site 17, p. 60). The Corps disbanded for the third and last time in 1853.

Return to the footbridge and continue east upriver 420 metres till you reach a sign on the left indicating the former Merri Creek Protectorate Station (Melway 2D E6) before you reach Hubert Olney Oval. The Native Police camp and barracks were also in this vicinity.

Public transport: Alight at Victoria Park Station and then walk to site. Bus 201 travels from Lonsdale Street to the corner of Johnston Street and Trenerry Crescent.

Car parking: Trenerry Crescent car park, Abbotsford.

Cycling/walking trail: The Yarra Trail heads east towards Studley Park and west to the city; alternatively the Merri Creek Trail heads north to Coburg.

FACILITIES

Dights Falls is an attractive park with tables and shelter, weir and falls and a below-ground view of the Dights Mill water race. Yarra Bend Park has 260 hectares of bushland and recreation spaces with scenic walking trails, picnic grounds, river views and bird life.

TIME 1–2 hours.

FURTHER INFORMATION

Tel: 13 1963
Web: www.parkweb.vic.gov.au

DESCRIPTION

DESCRIPTION

Bolin Bolin Billabong and surrounding lagoons was one of the great ceremonial and meeting places of the Wurundjeri and the site of the annual eel hunting season. A cultural interpretation trail prepared by the Wurundjeri Council tells the history of the Wurundjeri people.

LOCATION

175 Bullen Road, Bulleen. Access is from an unmarked drive on the west side of Bulleen Road, 300 metres north of the Veneto Club. Melway: 32 C–D8.

GETTING THERE

Public transport: From Heidelberg Station on the Hurstbridge line take bus 291 to the corner of Manningham and Bulleen Roads.

Cycling/walking: The nearest access to the main Yarra Trail (at Banksia Park) is at Banksia Bridge and Street. The trail proceeds south through Yarra Flats Park or north to Banyule Flats Reserve.

Car parking: Bullen Road, or nearby at Bulleen Park. Melway: 32 C9.

TIME 1 hour.

Bolin Bolin Billabong, one of the great ceremonial and meeting places of the Wurundjeri.

SITE 15
Bolin Bolin Billabong

The suburb of Bulleen draws its name from the Bolin Bolin wetlands. Bolin Bolin Billabong was once part of a large network of lagoons, and an important willam for the Wurundjeri clans and by invitation, other clans of the Kulin nation. During these gatherings, initiations and ceremonies could be conducted, marriages arranged, goods traded, and disputes settled. The Assistant Protector William Thomas recorded many visits by the Kulin to Bolin including in August 1840, March 1841, December 1843, November 1845 and June 1848.

Gatherings in late summer and autumn could last for weeks as the annual eel migration provided an abundant source of food. The site also had religious and cultural significance.

Bolin Bolin is a delightful, almost secret location which contains rare and threatened species of fauna and flora not found elsewhere in the Yarra River corridor, including one of the most intact remnant River Red Gum wetland habitats.

Signage along the trail provides a cultural interpretation of the Wurunderi people and their successful struggle for self-determination.

ACTIVITIES

The Bolin Bolin Cultural Landscape Trail runs along the Yarra River past the Bolin Bolin Billabong from Bulleen Park to Heide Museum of Modern Art passing Banksia Park, Bulleen Art and Garden and the Veneto Club. A scarred tree (Site 16) is located in the Museum car park.

FURTHER INFORMATION

Parks Victoria
Tel: 13 1963
Web: www.parkweb.vic.gov.au

Maningham City Council
Tel: (03) 9840 9333
Web: www.manningham.vic.gov.au

One giant, sprawling tree is estimated to be several hundred years old. Long-necked turtles, a favourite Kulin food, have been found breeding in the billabong.

During the 1840s, the Kulin were increasingly forced to seek government charity as their sources of bush foods were cut off by the sale of their lands. In 1841, Assistant Protector William Thomas pointed out in vain that the sale of Bolin Bolin would drastically cut the food supply of the Wurundjeri clans, 'when Bolin and the few lagoons adjacent becomes private property it will be one of the most serious losses experienced by the blacks'.

Today, Bolin Bolin remains a place of spiritual and cultural inspiration to the Wurundjeri people. In the park, a walking trail of nine sites with signage displaying paintings and cultural interpretation tells the story of the Wurundjeri people and their successful struggle for self-determination.

DESCRIPTION

One of Melbourne's finest scarred trees is located in the grounds of the Heide Museum of Modern Art, near the western end of the car park.

LOCATION

7 Templestowe Road, Bulleen. Melway: 32 E5.

GETTING THERE

Public transport: From Heidelberg Station, take bus 291 to the corner of Manningham and Bulleen Roads.

Cycling/walking: The nearest access to the main Yarra Trail (at Banksia Park) is at Banksia Street. Melway: 32 C5.

TIME 30 minutes

FACILITIES

Gift shop and cafe. Cafe open Tuesday to Friday 10am–5pm and Saturday to Sunday 9am–5pm. Admission charges apply to the Gallery, open Tuesday–Sunday 10am–5pm. Accessible toilets.

FURTHER INFORMATION

Tel: (03) 9850 1500
Web: www.heide.com.au

SITE 16
Heide Museum, scarred tree

The Yarra River Valley in eastern Melbourne contains sites of great spiritual power for the Kulin. Its wild beauty and power also inspired artists such as the Heidelberg School in the 1890s and the Heide Circle modernists in the 1940s. Today the Heide property, a former dairy farm, is home to Melbourne's Museum of Modern Art. In 1934, it was purchased by John and Sunday Reed who had broad intellectual interests in art, politics, literature, poetry and gardening and created a haven for artists such as Albert Tucker and Sydney Nolan. Nolan used the techniques of Indigenous Australians and painters to create his giant Eureka Stockade mural which is in the foyer of the Reserve Bank of Australia building in the city centre.

The presence of the traditional owners of Heide is marked by one of Melbourne's best known scarred trees located in the car park. The large River Red Gum, estimated to be several hundred years old, is of particular significance to the Wurundjeri people. It is one of three scarred trees in the area. Stone flint tools have also been unearthed at Heide.

Scarred trees indicate the presence of camp sites and bear the marks resulting from the removal of bark by Aboriginal people, in most cases before European settlement. The removal of a deep cutting of bark from Heide's tree may have been for housing, a shield, a water container or ritual boards. Foot holds were also cut into trees to gain access to lookout points, possums, bee nests and bark higher up the tree.

To remove the bark, Aboriginal people cut an outline of the desired shape, usually with stone axes. The bark was then levered off. On the Heide tree, axe marks at the base of the scar are covered by regrowth which is typical of scarred trees that are especially old. Unfortunately, many are now disappearing as a result of natural ageing, clearing or fire. There have been over 700 scarred trees reported in Melbourne. These trees provide Aboriginal people with an important link to their heritage.

The scarred tree in the grounds of the Heide Museum of Modern Art.

On 1 June 2013, the tree, hundreds of years old, was honoured with the name 'Yingabeal' by Wurundjeri Elder Bill Nicolson senior in a public ceremony at Heide. The Wurundjeri believe that Yingabeal is at the junction point of five traditional Wurundjeri travel and trade routes known as 'Songlines' and is likely the most important such marker tree still existing in Victoria.

DESCRIPTION

The Dandenong Police Paddocks Reserve is an important cultural site where the main headquarters of the Native Police Corps and the Port Phillip Aboriginal Protectorate Station were located.

LOCATION

Corner Brady Road and Baden Powell Drive, Endeavour Hills. Melway: 81 H11.

GETTING THERE

The Dandenong Police Paddocks Reserve is 30 kilometres southeast of Melbourne. The main access is from Brady Road which leads to the Nerre Nerre Warren Picnic Area (Melway: 82 A11). From there a walking trail marked 'Historic Area and Viewing Platform' leads 1.3 km to the location of the former Protectorate Station, Native Police Corps and Police Stud Depot (Melway: 81 K9). There are views over the historic Aboriginal reserve.

HOURS Open at 10am but closing times vary according to daylight savings.

TIME 60–90 minutes.

Above: Site of the Dandenong Police Paddocks Reserve.

SITE 17
Dandenong Police Paddocks Reserve

The Dandenong Police Paddocks Reserve is a large public parkland adjoining Dandenong Creek. Covering 499 hectares, it contains native forest, cultural sites, walking trails and sporting venues. The area is an important wildlife corridor and home to species such as the sugar glider (a type of possum), Powerful Owl, swamp scrub communities and native fish in the bordering Dandenong Creek.

The park is also one of Melbourne's most significant heritage places and of great spiritual and historical importance to the Kulin before and after European settlement. The Kulin knew the location as Nerre Nerre Werren, a place for camping, ceremonies and exchange on the border of their clan territories. On 5 September 1840, it was chosen in consultation with the Woiwurrung and Boon Wurrung people for Melbourne's first Protectorate Station after the Chief Protector requested they find a mutually agreeable reserve.

The Port Phillip Aboriginal Protectorate Station (1840–42) was an early attempt to move the Kulin away from their hunter–gatherer culture into the sedentary non-Aboriginal settler life and 'protect' them from the ills of civilisation. School classes and religious services were organised and rations were exchanged for manual labour.

FACILITIES

The picnic area at the end of Brady Road has barbecue and picnicking facilities, shelter, toilets and parking.

OTHER ACTIVITIES

The reserve has a diverse combination of rural bushland, cultural heritage and sporting areas with recreational opportunities for walkers, cyclists, bird watchers, dog owners, golfers and athletes. There are lead and off-lead dog areas.

FURTHER INFORMATION

Tel: 13 1963
Web: www.parkweb.vic.gov.au

Cohunguiam and Munight, Aboriginal policemen, William Strutt, 1851. State Library of Victoria, H88.21/112.

Nerre Nerre Warren was also the original base of the Native Police Corps headquarters in 1837–39 under Christiaan de Villiers, and later under Henry Dana in 1842–52. Between these two periods they were located at Merri Creek (see Site 14, p. 54). The commanders such as Dana made allowances for the men's cultural and kinship responsibilities. The men of the Corps hunted fish in Dandenong Creek and cultivated gardens at the Station.

The site later became home to the Victorian Police Horse Stud Depot. Many Aboriginal men who worked as police trackers were based here 1879–31. A celebrated achievement of trackers was when three young children of the Duff family were lost for nine days in the Victorian Wimmera in 1864. After the trackers were called in, the children were all found within a day.

There are historic features in the northwest area of the park associated with different periods of occupation. The Nerre Nerre Warren Protectorate Station is now one of the few physical remains of nineteenth century Aboriginal reserves in Victoria.

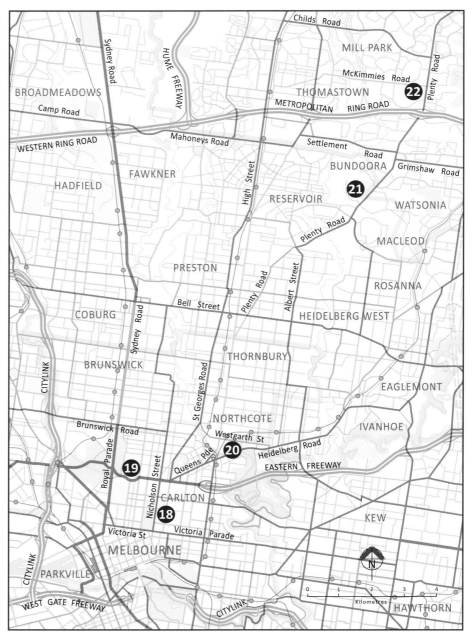

Map of sites 18–22.

Moreton Bay Fig Tree, Carlton Gardens. Photograph by Hari Ho.

INNER NORTH

These are traditional lands of the Woiwurrung, today under the cultural custodianship of the Wurundjeri Tribe Land and Compensation Cultural Heritage Council. The area holds many and varied historic and archaeological places of immense importance. Bundoora Park and Hall Reserve, Merri Creek are located within ancient red gum woodlands that were rich sources of wildlife, fresh water and traditional materials. Merri Creek was one of Victoria's greatest meeting places for Aboriginal people in the 1840s for the purpose of exchange, ceremony and law business. Fitzroy became the centre of urban Aboriginal community life, revival and self-determination from the 1920s.

SITES

18. Fitzroy Aboriginal heritage walking trail

19. Derrimut gravestone

20. Hall Reserve, Merri Creek

    Of interest: Melbourne Treaty site

21. Bundoora scarred tree

22. Keelbundoora scarred tree and Heritage Trail

DESCRIPTION

A self-guided trail marked by prominent plaques on locations in the suburb of Fitzroy, which became an important social and political hub of Aboriginal Melbourne from the 1920s.

LOCATION

The trail begins at the Moreton Bay Fig Tree in the Carlton Gardens at the corner of Nicholson and Gertrude Streets and extends along Gertrude Streets and surrounding streets.
Melway: 2B K11, 2C A–D11.

GETTING THERE

Transport options include tram 86 or 96 to the corner of Nicholson and Gertrude Streets, Free City Circle Tram to Victoria Parade, city loop train to Parliament Station, bus routes 250, 251 and 402 to Rathdowne Street and free City of Melbourne Tourist Shuttle Bus to stop No. 4.

TIME Up to 2 hours.

FURTHER INFORMATION

An excellent walking guide map and phone app are available from the City of Yarra. Maps are also available from the Visitors Centre, Federation Square.

Tel: (03) 9205 5555
Web: www.yarracity.vic.gov.au.

The Moreton Bay Fig Tree, a meeting place for legendary Aboriginal activists. Photograph by Hari Ho.

SITE 18
Fitzroy Aboriginal heritage walking trail

The inner city suburb of Fitzroy is renowned for its heritage architecture and its vibrant community life of artists, musicians, cafes and festivals. However, like Redfern in Sydney, Fitzroy also has a distinguished history of civil rights campaigns and self-determination by Aboriginal people though the creation of radical political, social, sporting, music and cultural movements. From the 1920s, as rural missions were closed in favour of the government's assimilation policy, Koories moved to the city in search of work. The Aboriginal community of Melbourne gradually increased and many found their home among family and friends in Fitzroy. A popular name for Fitzroy's Gertrude Street was 'The Black Mile'.

By the 1950s, Fitzroy supported a community of more than 300 Koories, with many living in surrounding inner city suburbs. Fitzroy was not just the largest Aboriginal community in Victoria but also the social and political hub of Aboriginal Melbourne. The leaders of the Fitzroy community and the successful organisations they created around Gertrude Street profoundly influenced political and cultural reform in Australia.

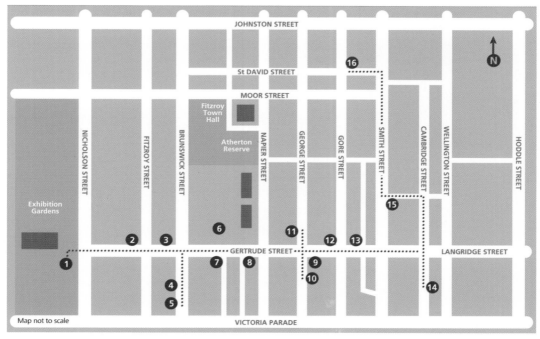

Map of the Fitzroy Aboriginal heritage walking trail. Courtesy the City of Yarra.

On 5 February 2009, well-known singer–songwriter Archie Roach performed songs, inspired by his time in Fitzroy, to launch the City of Yarra's self-guided trail of fifteen bronze plaques commemorating the area's Aboriginal history. The trail begins at the 'Speakers' Moreton Bay Fig Tree in Carlton Gardens and finishes at the former church of Pastor Doug Nicholls in Gore Street.

Route

1. The Moreton Bay Fig Tree, Carlton Gardens was a meeting place where legendary Aboriginal activists addressed public gatherings in the 1920–40s (see p. 68). **Location**: Nicholson Street, Carlton.

2. The Koori Club, established by artist Lin Onus, was an influential social and political meeting place during the 1960s for young Aboriginal activists. **Location**: 43 Gertrude Street, Fitzroy.

Site of the Koori Club. Photograph by Hari Ho.

The Atherton Gardens. Photograph by Hari Ho.

3. The Aboriginal Housing Board of Victoria began its fight in 1981 to provide safe, secure and affordable housing that met the cultural needs of Aboriginal tenants. **Location**: 79 Gertrude Street, Fitzroy.

4. The Victorian Aboriginal Legal Service officially commenced in 1973 after the community took lawyers to a local pub to witness police indiscriminately arresting Aboriginal people. **Location**: 11 Brunswick Street, Fitzroy.

5. The Victorian Aboriginal Child Care Agency was established in 1976 in response to the effects of racist government practices and policies regarding Aboriginal children, families and communities. **Location**: 5 Brunswick Street, Fitzroy.

6. The Atherton Gardens Housing Estate park was a popular meeting place for vulnerable Koories in the 1980s including singer–songwriter Archie Roach. **Location**: Corner of Gertrude and Napier Streets, Fitzroy.

7. The Koori Information Centre was established in the early 1980s to meet a rising groundswell of community interest in Aboriginal issues. **Location**: 120 Gertrude Street, Fitzroy.

8. The Victorian Aboriginal Health Service which opened in 1973 was revolutionary. It was the first Aboriginal community-controlled health and dental service in Victoria. It responded to the growing number of Koories who needed medical attention, but were reluctant to go to mainstream medical services. **Location**: 229 Gertrude Street (1973–79)and 136 Gertrude Street (1979–93), Fitzroy.

9. The Fitzroy Stars Aboriginal Community Youth Club Gymnasium was formed in 1977 by the Victorian Aboriginal Health Service and has been central to the lives of countless young people. **Location**: 184–186 Gertrude Street, Fitzroy.

10. The George Wright Hostel was established in 1974 as a half-way house and shelter in response to the many homeless Koorie men in and around Fitzroy. **Location**: 66 George Street, Fitzroy.

11. The Nindeebiya Workshop established in 1983 as a community hub where Aboriginal people could gather safely to practise arts and crafts and play sports. It opened early and

The Fitzroy Stars Aboriginal Community Youth Club Gymansium. Photograph by Hari Ho.

served breakfast for the 'street mob' and 'Parkies'. **Location**: 99 George Street, Fitzroy.

12. The Builders Arms Hotel was a key Aboriginal social and political meeting place in the 1940–80s together with other hotels along and around Gertrude Street including the Napier, the Rob Roy and the Royal. **Location**: 211 Gertrude Street, Fitzroy.

13. The Victorian Aboriginal Health Service, see 8, p. 66.

14. Koori Kollij, first opened at 56 Cunningham Street, Northcote in March 1984 but moved the following December to Collingwood. At first an Aboriginal studies course, it quickly became an Aboriginal health worker training program that forged new and enduring standards of Aboriginal healthcare in Australia. **Location**: 42 Cambridge Street, Collingwood.

15. The Victorian Aboriginal Co-operative Limited was established in 1976 and provided local housing and welfare services to the Aboriginal community of Melbourne. It initiated the establishment of at least fifteen important other community-controlled services. **Location**: 108 Smith Street, Collingwood.

16. The site of the Aboriginal Church of Christ is where Pastor Doug Nicholls and his wife Gladys Nicholls established the Church in 1943 and it attracted a devoted following. Sir Doug became Governor of South Australia in 1976. **Location**: 258 Gore Street, Fitzroy.

Pastor Doug Nicholls and congregation, Church of Christ, Gore Street, Fitzroy. Photograph by Richard Seeger, Nicholas family collection. Courtesy Pam Pederson.

ACTIVISTS WHO CHANGED ABORIGINAL MELBOURNE

A Moreton Bay Fig tree in the 1920–40s was the unlikely gathering place for political reformers such as Jack Patten, Bill Onus, William Cooper, Ebenezer Lovett, Martha Nevin and Margaret Tucker to address crowds and debate Aboriginal issues.

In the 1960s artist Lin Onus established the Koori Club to foster new political and social ideas that inspired young activists through the leadership of Bruce McGuiness and the club's Koorier newspaper. Before the Victorian Aboriginal Legal Service began in 1973, legal services were provided by volunteers including Stewart Murray, Les Booth, Alick and Merle Jackomos, Hyllus Maris, Margaret (Briggs) Wirrapunda, Dan Atkinson, Jim Berg, Julia Jones and Geraldine Briggs. Ron Merkel QC, Gareth Evans QC, Ron Castan AM QC, Peter Hanks QC, and Dr Elizabeth Eggleston provided legal advice as well. It was also in 1973 that community members such as Julia

Jones, Margaret Tucker, Edna Brown, Bruce McGuinness and Alma Thorpe pioneered the Victorian Aboriginal Health Service to provide quality health care.

Activist Robbie Thorpe created the famous 'Pay the Rent' campaign and was the leader of the Koori Information Centre where the Koorier was produced and where Lin Onus produced striking comic books and t-shirts. Jock Austin was the first staff member of the legendary Fitzroy Stars Gymnasium in Gertrude Street, initiated to combat drug and alcohol problems, by Alma Thorpe, Bruce McGuiness, Dr Bill Roberts, Jock Austin, John 'Longfulla' Austin, Johnny Mac, Bindi Jack, Ronnie 'Fox' Foster, 'Punchy' Rose and 'Magpie'. The George Wright Hostel was named for one of Fitzroy's 'lane boys', a homeless man and a well-known local identity. In George Street in the 1980s, the Nindeebiya workshop staff including Jan Chessels, Maxine Briggs and Jack Charles generously offered a friendly smile and welcoming hand to anyone in need.

DOUGLAS AND GLADYS NICHOLLS

Both Doug and Gladys worked at local, state and national levels to improve the economic wellbeing and civil rights of Aboriginal people, including campaigning for the 1967 Referendum as part of the Victorian chapter. Their work touched on the lives of many and, from their humble beginnings at the Gore Street Mission in Fitzroy to Government House in Adelaide, their legacy still lives on today. They pressed the case for Aboriginal reconciliation well before it became a popular movement and provided comfort and assistance to many people who were homeless or desperate.

Douglas Nicholls, KCVO, OBE (1906–88) was the first Aboriginal person to be knighted. He served as Governor of South Australia in 1976–77. His beginnings were humble. He was born on Cummeragunja Reserve, New South Wales in Yorta Yorta country. At the age of eight, he saw his older sister, Hilda, forcibly removed by police to a domestic training home. By thirteen he was working with his uncle as a tar boy and general hand on sheep stations. His athletic prowess eventually brought him to the Fitzroy Football Club and the Victorian interstate team. He toured with Jimmy Sharman's Boxing Troupe and won the Warracknabeal Gift foot race. During the Second World War he enlisted then later he worked as social worker and minister in the Fitzroy Aboriginal community dealing with alcohol abuse, gambling and conflict with the police. He later became the pastor of the first Aboriginal Church of Christ that he and Gladys founded in Gore Street.

As a field officer for the Aborigines Advancement League which he helped to establish in 1957, Nicholls drew Aboriginal issues to public notice, set up hostels for

Dungula Warmayirr (River People) in Melbourne's Parliament Gardens Reserve in Spring Street, is a tribute to Sir Douglas and Lady Gladys Nicholls. It was unveiled in 2007.

Aboriginal children and was a founding member of the Federal Council for the Advancement of Aborigines and Torres Strait Islanders. He was always passionate about the dignity of the individual which he exemplified in his own behaviour and his concern for others.

Lady Gladys Nicholls (1906–81) was a leading activist whose community service and commitment to advancing Aboriginal rights was an inspiration to many, as well as being an important role model for young women. The third of six children, she was also born on Cummeragunja Reserve. After her husband, Herbert Nicholls, tragically died, she later married his brother, Douglas. They became partners in both life and work. Her name was inscribed on the Victorian government's Victorian Women's Honour Roll in 2008.

The life and work of two of Australia's most prominent Aboriginal leaders were immortalised in this important memorial.

Location: Parliament Gardens Reserve, Corner Spring Street and Albert Road, Melbourne. Melway: 2F K1.

INNER NORTH

Derrimut, oil painting, Benjamin Duterrau, 1837. Mitchell Library, State Library of New South Wales.

SITE 19
Derrimut gravestone

The relationship between the Melbourne clans and colonists in the first months of settlement in 1835 was cooperative. Boon Wurrrung Arweet (clan leader) Derrimut, even warned the settlers of an impending attack by hostile clans from outside Melbourne. On 3 December 1835, founding settler John Fawkner wrote in his diary, 'Derramuck came this day and told us that the natives intended to rush down upon us and plunder our goods and murder us, we cleaned our pieces and prepared for them…I and two others chased the Blacks away some distance'.

Benbow and Billibellary, who were also clan leaders of the Kulin, acted to protect the new settlement too. These Kulin leaders may have believed that the Melbourne Treaty or Tanderrum ritual with John Batman in June 1835 had given the settlers protection as well as visiting rights to their territory.

Derrimut and John Fawkner became close friends. In April 1836, Fawkner wrote that Derrimut, 'a chief from whom with others I bought my land, live with me, and frequently go out and shoot kangaroos, snakes for me'. When the colonists learned that Derrimut's wife had been abducted by whalers, they went to considerable efforts to return her but were unsuccessful. In August 1836, Derrimut travelled with Fawkner to Tasmania, where Derrimut was presented to Governor Arthur, received a uniform and had his portrait painted.

Subsequent events showed Derrimut's faith in his friendship with leading settlers to be ill-founded. Several years later and disillusioned, he protested to merchant William Hull:

> Why me have lubra [wife]? Why me have piccaninny [children]? You have all this place...all this mine, all along Derrimut's once,...no good have children, no good have lubra, me tumble down and die very soon now.

The gratitude expressed on his gravestone after his death was not expressed in the latter years of Derrimut's life. In July 1863, the government announced the sale of the last of his traditional lands at Mordialloc, despite his protests and the efforts of Assistant Protector William Thomas. Derrimut's health rapidly declined with the loss of the last of his country and he died on 26 April 1864 (see Site 32, p. 120).

Derrimut's gravestone.

Derrimut was an influential if controversial cultural intermediary. In a tumultuous era, he not only earned, but on occasion demanded the respect of leading settlers. He campaigned for his people in his vocal criticism of dispossession and in his advocacy for Mordialloc Reserve. Above all, Derrimut was always vividly his own person, making his own choices to maintain a sphere of influence in a volatile world. A Melbourne suburb, street, park and electoral district preserve his name and memory.

DESCRIPTION

Troops attacked a large Aboriginal gathering on Heidelberg Road near Merri Creek in 1840 resulting in mass arrest and imprisonment as well as the death of two well-known Aboriginal men.

LOCATION

Heidelberg Road, Clifton Hill, beside Merri Creek along the Merri Creek Trail. Melway: 30 G12. The attack occurred in Hall Reserve or George Knott Reserve, the parks located on the south and north sides of Heidelberg Road, near Heidelberg Road Bridge.

GETTING THERE

Public Transport: Westgarth Railway Station is within ten minutes walk.

Cycling/walking: Hall Reserve is on the Merri Creek Trail which links to the Yarra Trail further south.

Above: *Windberry*, pencil sketch by William Thomas. Woiwurrung clan leader Windberry was one of two Kulin killed as a result of a police raid while Kulin clans met for ceremonial business.

SITE 20
Hall Reserve, Merri Creek

Every weekend families in the suburb of Clifton Hall enjoy the lawns, playgrounds and bike paths of the peaceful Hall Reserve near the Heidelberg Bridge. However, on 11 October 1840, Aboriginal families awoke in terror as a large party of police and troopers rode into their campsite at early dawn, waving guns and swords. Weeping and fearful, the men, women and children were marched by the soldiers to the stockade in Melbourne where they were imprisoned.

About 300 Kulin from different clans had assembled in Melbourne for ceremonial and cultural business near Heidelberg Road beside Merri Creek. Heidelberg Road is at the northern neck of the loop or island created by the encircling Yarra and Merri waterways. This 'island' known as Yarra Bend was a very popular willam for Kulin gatherings in the 1840s.

The raid by Major Samuel Lettsom of the 80th Regiment was the outcome of increasing tension as the Kulin, especially outside Melbourne, began to actively resist the increasing occupation of their lands by settlers and the destruction of their food and water sources by stock. Lettsom was searching

Left: Hall Reserve.

for 'troublemakers' from the Taungurong clans from the Goulburn River area and an exasperated Superintendent La Trobe had approved the raid.

Two leading men, Windberry and Neruknerbook, were killed as a result of the raid. All but thirty Kulin who were arrested were released the same day. Ten were convicted after trial, but nine later escaped during transport down the Yarra River. In a subsequent hearing, Judge Willis declared the trial of those convicted to have been illegal.

Assistant Protector William Thomas wrote: 'Windberry was one of the noblest minded blacks I ever met with – he had saved the lives of many shepherds and travellers on the Goulbourn River and deserved a much better fate. He had the courage when Major Lettsom surrounded the blacks to step forward and ask what they were going to do raising his *wadi* (club) at the time. One police man shot him dead.'

The attack was a pivotal event in black and white relations in Melbourne. The Aboriginal Protectors reported that Kulin leaders were infuriated and were threatening revenge by retreating to the mountains to 'drive the white fellows from the country'. They also channelled their anger into sorcery to call up the dreaded Mindye the rainbow serpent, to inflict disaster on the Europeans.

Batman's Treaty with the Aborigines at Merri Creek, 6th June 1835 by John Wesley Burtt. State Library of Victoria, H92.196.

MELBOURNE TREATY SITE

'This (Treaty signing) took place alongside of a beautiful stream of water, and from whence my land commences, and where a tree is marked four ways to know the corner boundary.' — John Batman's journal, 6 June 1835.

The exact location of the signing of John Batman's treaty known as the 'Grant of the Territory called Dutigalla' or the 'Melbourne Treaty', has long been debated with the Merri, Darebin and Edgar creeks as suggested sites. In 1835, John Batman, a grazier from Tasmania, claimed that eight Aboriginal 'chiefs' signed over 600,000 acres of land in consideration of blankets, mirrors and axes, plus an annual tribute or rent to be paid to the Kulin.

The traditional claim has been that the treaty took place on the banks of Merri Creek, opposite today's Rushall Station near McLachlan and Walker Streets, Northcote. A former memorial plinth was discovered a short distance upstream from there in 2004. In recent years a damaged Aboriginal scarred tree was still standing in McLaren Street. Ian Hunter, a Wurundjeri elder, recalls that in 2007, his grandmother, Martha Nevin, told stories about

his great-great-great-grandfather Jerum-Jerum, one of the senior tribal elders at the Treaty signing. 'Nanna pointed out the scar tree and said, "That's where it happened".'

The well-known Wurundjeri leader at Coranderrk Aboriginal Station, William Barak, told anthropologist Alfred Howitt that he was present as a boy at the treaty and that his father Bebejern and his uncles Billibellary, Bungarie, Cooloolock and Jaga Jaga were participants.

The agreement was negotiated with clan leaders in a Tanderrum ritual which provided permission for temporary access to the land by a ritual exchange of gifts. Batman ignored the fact that Aboriginal land, with its sacred responsibilities and relationships, could not be bought or sold. However, the Melbourne Treaty remains unique in early Australia in that it recognised Aboriginal title to land, a view endorsed by the High Court of Australia 157 years later in what is known as the 'Mabo Case' — *Mabo v Queensland* (No. 2) (1992) (see p. 16).

Despite the treaty, Batman's claim on behalf of a Tasmanian land syndicate to have purchased

Left: Present day view of the possible Treaty signing site on the banks of the Merri Creek.
Right: The Batman deed, 1835. State Library of Victoria, MS 13484.

Melbourne and Geelong for 200 pounds worth of goods was dismissed by the New South Wales colonial government three months later. The British declared that all land was terra nullius (unoccupied) to ensure it could only be sold by the Crown. However, it did legitimise settlement in Melbourne by agreeing to cease confining settlers to the limits of existing colonies. This sparked perhaps the greatest land rush in history. Within four years of the treaty, more Aboriginal land was seized by settlers in Australia than in the preceding fifty. The Treaty, which started with vows of friendship and cooperation, became the trigger for the destruction of Kulin traditional society.

James Boyce describes the background to the Melbourne Treaty in his book, *1835: The Founding of Melbourne and the Conquest of Australia* (see Reference list, p. 138).

Location: Rushall Station is located on the Epping line beside the Merri Creek. Melway: 30 D11. A high footbridge with excellent views stretches over the creek to the opposite bank.

POLITICS OF THE TREATY

Tanderrum was a powerful Kulin ceremony of hospitality and friendship toward strangers usually facilitated by intermediaries. The three Europeans in Batman's party were skilled mediators from the Black Wars in Tasmania. Their agreement with the Kulin was as much psychological as formal. They also brought seven Sydney natives with them led by John Pigeon as cultural intermediaries who impressed the Kulin clans. In fact the Kulin offered young wives to these men, in effect making the men their relatives.

The Kulin had been subjected to forty years of sporadic landings, shootings and abductions by whalers and visiting expeditions. The treaty was an opportunity for an alliance with a small group of enthusiastic strangers who sought visiting rights in exchange for regular payments of goods which included amazing new technologies. They were unaware that Batman would represent this to the British as a private land purchase. Neither party in the alliance realised that the British response would trigger an eventual mass wave of settlers. The Kulin continued to demand the treaty obligations be filled, leading to confrontations and incorrect accusations that the Kulin were seeking handouts. During Aboriginal demonstrations in Melbourne today, people still occasionally hold up the banner: Pay the Rent!

Aboriginal police trackers were employed at the depot from 1931. From left: Norman Brown, Albert Prince, Dippo Powder, Christie Munda, Bertie Baker, Archie Napoleon Bonaparte and George Rigby; two men far right unidentified.

DESCRIPTION

Bundoora Park is a 180-hectare reserve, offering a great diversity of interests including scarred trees, a Wurundjeri plant garden, an historic Aboriginal trackers hut, and an extraordinary lookout over Melbourne. Some of Melbourne's oldest trees can be found in the woodlands near the entrance to the park.

LOCATION

The main entrance to the park is at 1069 Plenty Road, Bundoora. Melway: 19 F4. The Bundoora Homestead is at 7–27 Snake Gully Drive, Bundoora.

GETTING THERE

Public transport: Tram 86 from Bourke Street to stop 61.

Car parking: Available in the park.

Cycling/walking trail: The Darebin Creek Trail runs ten kilometres from the park to the main Yarra River Trail.

HOURS

Park: Sunrise to Sunset. Visitors Centre: 8.30am–5pm (cafe 10am–4pm), Coopers Settlement: 10am–4.30pm.

SITE 21
Bundoora scarred tree

Bundoora Park is Melbourne's most varied park. It includes landscapes and buildings which represent occupation from prior to settlement to the present day. There are marsupials and birdlife, ancient woodlands used by the Kulin, lakes, a colonial farm and homestead, and a police remount depot used by Aboriginal police trackers.

The park is in the former estate of the Wurundjeri willam clan. Large River Red Gums, hundreds of years old, thrive among rolling grassland, some bearing marks from Aboriginal use for shelters and utensils. East of Bramham Drive opposite Waters Way is an Aboriginal scarred tree surrounded by a steel picket fence. Outcrops of silcrete can be found around Mount Cooper in the park. These were quarried by Aboriginal people to produce flaked stone tools.

The AH Capp Drive passes the Visitors Centre on route to Mount Cooper, which is the highest point in metropolitan Melbourne, and has outstanding views. It would have provided the Kulin with an ideal view to locate other clans by smoke rising from their camp fires.

Coopers Settlement, which is accessed via the Visitors Centre, contains a wildlife reserve with kangaroos and emus, a Wurundjeri plant garden, and a pioneer farm. It also contains a rare police trackers' hut circa 1920s that housed Aboriginal police trackers from Queensland in 1930–51. It is a prefabricated railway hut, simply furnished. Queensland trackers were used regularly in Victoria between 1880 and the 1960s, the best known occasion being the pursuit of the bushranger Ned Kelly.

The first settlers used Bundoora Park as a homestead for grazing cattle, sheep and horses. The Bundoora Homestead built by John Smith on Mount Cooper in 1889 is now a public art gallery, cafe and gardens.

ADMISSION

Entry to the Park, Visitors Centre and Bundoora Homestead are free. Entry fees apply for Coopers Settlement including the Heritage Village, Wildlife Reserve and Wurundjeri Garden.

TIME 1–2 hours.

OTHER ACTIVITIES

There are picnic grounds with playgrounds and toilets.

FURTHER INFORMATION

Bundoora Park
Tel: (03) 8470 8170
Web: www.bundoorapark.com.au

Bundoora Homestead Art Centre
Tel: (03) 9496 1060
Web: www.bundoora homestead.com

The police trackers' hut, c. 1920s.

DESCRIPTION

A self-guided trail, marked by decorative poles and signage, through a red gum woodland rich in scarred and ancient trees surrounding a modern university campus.

LOCATION

RMIT University Bundoora west campus, 225–245 Plenty Road, Bundoora. Melway: 9 J8.

GETTING THERE

Although marker 1 is outside building 202 (RMIT bookshop), it can be simpler to commence at markers 2, 3 and 4 near the lake at the northwest end of the eastern carpark and follow the trail west towards Betula Avenue.

Public Transport: Tram route 86 runs from the City to the RMIT Bundoora west campus. Bus services operate from local train stations to the Bundoora campus.

Car parking: Metered parking is available on campus at the eastern carpark off Clements Drive via Plenty Road.

FACILITIES

Cafeterias and public toilets are available on the campus.

The Possum Tree, Stop 3 of the Keelbundoora Scarred Tree and Heritage Trail. Photograph courtesy RMIT University.

SITE 22
Keelbundoora Scarred Tree and Heritage Trail

The name of the suburb of Bundoora derives from Keelbundoora, the name of a young boy present at the signing of the Melbourne Treaty. The Royal Melbourne Institute of Technology's Bundoora campus contains a large population of remnant River Red Gums including six scarred trees that are rare and fragile reminders of the resource harvesting techniques practiced by hundreds of generations of Aboriginal and Torres Strait Islander people across Australia.

In 2008, Friends of Bundoora Red Gums was formed and held their first planting day with RMIT staff, students and local community members to plant 400 local indigenous plants to protect and enhance the health of the magnificent River Red Gums on campus.

The Keelbundoora Scarred Tree and Heritage Trail was first proposed by the RMIT Student Services Group and the RMIT

ADMISSION Free.

HOURS 8.30am–5pm.

TIME 1 hour.

FURTHER INFORMATION

Ngarara Willim Centre
Tel: 1800 054 885 or
(03) 9925 4885
Email: info@ngarara.william@
rmit.edu.au
Web: www.rmit.edu.au/ngarara

Walking maps website
www.walkingmaps.com.au/
walk/119

The starting point of the Keelbundoora Scarred Tree and Heritage Trail. Photograph courtesy RMIT University.

Ngarara Willim Centre to show due respect to the Wurundjeri people and their history on the land now occupied by the University. The Centre offers Aboriginal and Torres Strait Islander students ongoing guidance with study, living and cultural needs.

The tree scars tell us a great deal about the Wurundjeri clan, the traditional owners of much of the lands in and around Melbourne. The Wurundjeri Council and their representative Annette Xibberas helped develop the trail of twelve sites as well as the brochures and signage.

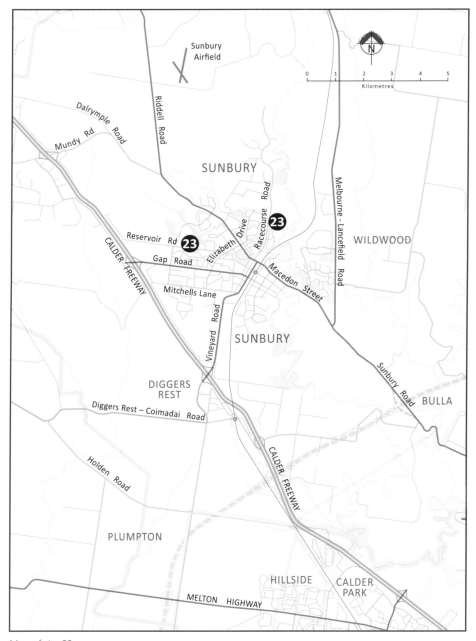

Map of site 23.

OUTER NORTH

On the northwest and northeast outskirts of Melbourne, there are three sites of immense cultural and historical significance to local Aboriginal people including rare ceremonial circles and an extraordinary quarry of international significance. The basalt plains to the west and northwest of Melbourne provided extensive grasslands that supported grazing animals such as kangaroos and wallabies as well as habitat for possums, bandicoots, reptiles and birds. Fish were trapped on numerous shallow waterways using weirs, traps, lures, spears and nets. Edible plants provided roots, sap and tubers. Sunbury was an area where the Kulin harvested large quantities of *murnong* (yam daisy tubers) which would have sustained large groups during gatherings to conduct important ceremonies.

To the northeast, the events that occurred at Coranderrk Aboriginal Station in the nineteenth century were an important forerunner of the successful civil rights movement that gained prominence from the 1930s and initiated reforms that still influence the cultural and political landscape of Aboriginal Australia today.

Jackson's Creek valley in Sunbury, the location of important ceremonial earth rings.

SITE

23. Sunbury earth rings

   Of interest: Wil-im-ee Moor-ring (Mount William quarry)

   Of interest: Coranderrk Aboriginal Station and Cemetery

DESCRIPTION

Five rare Aboriginal earth rings believed to have been for religious or ceremonial uses.

LOCATION

Locations include Wirilda Court (Melway: 362 F12), Fullwood Drive (Melway: 381 HI), Hopbush Avenue, Correa Way and north of the junction of Old Riddells Road and Riddells Road. Sunbury is located forty kilometres northwest of Melbourne's central business district in the City of Hume.

GETTING THERE

A fenced area containing one of the earth rings is accessible 70 metres east of the eastern end of Wirilda Court, Sunbury. The site offers a striking view of the Jackson Creek Valley. From a path thirty metres east of the fenced area you can view a second earth ring in the distance. It is located in a fenced square, 350 metres to the northeast. A fenced area containing a third earth ring can be found at 76 Fullwood Drive, Sunbury, several minutes drive away.

CONSIDERATIONS

Observe all fence security and signs. All Aboriginal cultural places and their artefacts in Victoria are protected by law.

Above: Sunbury earth ring. Courtesy Aboriginal Affairs Victoria.

SITE 23
Sunbury earth rings

Gatherings of Kulin clans in Melbourne often took place at locations with religious significance where sacred ceremonies such as initiations and totemic rites were performed. Evidence of these ceremonial places is very rare in Victoria. However, in 1978, five earth rings were identified northwest of Melbourne, near Sunbury. An archaeological excavation of one of the rings suggested that they may have been used for ceremonies, including the initiation of young men. Initiations were of great importance in Aboriginal society and involved secret ceremonies that could last for weeks. Circular grounds known as Bora Rings are known to have been created for these ceremonies in other eastern states.

The five earth rings are located on gently sloping sites in the valley of Jacksons Creek. The creek was a territory marker between the Woiwurrung clan estates of the Marin balug and Wurundjeri willam. The rings consist of shallow, circular hollows fifteen metres to twenty-five metres in diameter formed by the removal of topsoil which was then piled in a circular ridge.

In 2012, nine hectares of land containing the earth rings was formally handed over to the custodianship of the Wurundjeri Council by the federal government's Indigenous Land Corporation.

William Barak, possibly taken at Coranderrk, Victoria, 1900. Reproduced with permission from Museum Victoria (XP 2589).

THE INITIATION OF BARAK

Wurundjeri willam clan leader William Barak corresponded with anthropologist Alfred Howitt to provide details of Wurundjeri lore including initiations. In 1884, Howitt organised for Barak and other senior men in Victoria to travel to Gippsland to perform initiations for the first time in thirty years. Melbourne was one of nine places in Victoria where *jibauk* (initiation ceremonies) for young men were conducted. Assistant Protector William Thomas, described initiation activities he observed as the 'Ceremony of Tobbut'.

Howitt described jibauk ceremonies where the initiates lived 200–300 metres from the main camp behind a screen of tree boughs that had a large fire in front of it. They were taken there by their maternal uncles. The *Wirrarap* (Aboriginal healer) also supervised them. The initiates' heads were shaved. Mud was plastered over their heads and shoulders and a wide band of pipe clay was painted from ear to ear across their faces. A number of *branjep* (aprons worn by men to cover their private parts) collected from other men were tied around their waists. An initiate carried a bag around his neck in which he sought food from others in the camp. During the ceremony, he

was instructed in what foods were forbidden to him, at least until he earned privileges at an older age.

When the probation period involving numerous trials and rituals ended, the jibauk camp was gradually shifted closer to the main camp. Finally, each initiate was presented with a possum rug and, wearing full male costume, admitted to the camp among rejoicing, singing and dancing.

Barak himself was initiated by Ninggalobin, Poleorong and his uncle Billibellary, who were important Kulin leaders in the Melbourne area. European colonisation had caused disruptions to initiation ceremonies. In response, these three men gathered at South Yarra to induct Barak into sacred lore. He was presented with the symbols of manhood: the *gombert* (reed necklace) around his neck, strips of possum skin tied around his biceps, his branjep, and his *ilbi-jerri*, a sharp and narrow bone or nosepeg. In return Barak presented Billibellary with a possum skin cloak.

Barak succeeded to the role of clan leader of the Wurundjeri willam and was leader at the Coranderrk Aboriginal Station where, like his uncle before him, he was a strong advocate for his people.

Wil-im-ee Moor-ring (Mount William quarry)

The Mount William quarry at Lancefield is a large heritage site of international importance where Aboriginal people quarried greenstone from stone outcrops to make their axes.

> 'When neighbouring tribes wanted stone for tomahawks they sent a messenger to Billibellary to say they would take opossum rugs and other things if he would give them stone for them. Billibellary's father when he was alive split up the stones and give it away for presents such as rugs, weapons, ornaments, belts, necklaces — three pieces of stone were given for a possum rug. People sometimes give presents in advance to get stone bye and bye.' — William Barak's description to anthropologist Alfred Howitt circa 1884.

For perhaps thousands of years, Aboriginal people quarried the superb greenstone (volcanic diorite) from stone outcrops on what is now called Mount William to make their axes. The quarry was the centre of an extraordinary trading network that extended 700 kilometres up into New South Wales and also into South Australia.

These axes were highly prized and traded for goods such as possum skins and other valuable resources. The trade also had important social functions. It strengthened bonds between social groups and reinforced kinship links, as well as birthplace and ceremonial obligations. Access to the quarry required the permission of several elders such as Wurundjeri william clan leader Billibellary who inherited the rights (see p. 26).

Stone outcrops were fractured using fire alternated with cold water, and the stone was levered loose with fire-hardened poles. Using stone anvils as work benches, the stones would be fashioned into blanks. These were later sharpened into axe heads using abrasive sandstone to achieve a sharp edge. A large sandstone boulder with thirty-one grooves made by the sharpening of stone axes is located at Mount Macedon, thirty kilometres away. St Kilda foreshore was also recorded as a location for sandstone suitable for grinding axes.

The quarry site covered forty hectares and the vast number of scattered rock fragments among the anvil stones is testimony to the industry of the tool makers. Researcher Isabel McBryde estimated there were 268 mining pits, eighteen of which were several metres deep surrounded by at least thirty-four discrete flaking floors, with debris up to twenty metres in diameter including some featuring a central outcropping rock used as an anvil. The site is of international significance and is listed on the National Register of Important Cultural Places.

Top: Greenstone outcrop used to harvest stone for axes, Mount William quarry. Right: Stone flakes from quarrying activity, Mount William quarry.

In 2012, the Wurundjeri Council collected stone from the quarry to make axes with which to build a Koorong or canoe from a River Red Gum at Plenty Gorge to strengthen their traditional culture (see p. 50).

The quarry is seventy-eight kilometres north of Melbourne. Access to the quarry requires the permission of the Wurundjeri Council. Public excursions to the site are usually organised annually by the Council during the Lancefield Agricultural Show held in October. For further information contact the Wurundjeri Tribe Land Cultural Heritage Council Inc. on (03) 8673 0901.

GIVING BACK

On 23 October 2012, ceremonial fires of burning gum leaves welcomed 200 Kulin elders and guests to a special ceremony on Mount William. They were there to witness the federal Minister for Families, Community Services and Indigenous Affairs, the Hon. Jenny Macklin MP formally hand over the title of the Mount William axe quarry to the Wurundjeri people. Also present were the Macedon Ranges Council who had gifted the quarry land to the Federal Indigenous Land Corporation in 1997. The title to a 9.1 hectare property in Sunbury containing the ceremonial earth rings was also handed over. The Wurundjeri Tribe Land Cultural Heritage Council now own these lands permanently to ensure their preservation.

Wedge-tailed eagles circled overhead in clear skies as elder Bill Nicholson, accepted the land on behalf of the Wurundjeri community. He said it was a fitting omen that Bunjil the eagle had come to witness this historic return of his traditional country.

Professor Isabel McBryde from the Australian National University School of History, who pioneered groundbreaking research into Mount William over many years, spoke passionately about the benefits of research done in close collaboration between Aboriginal people, historians and archaeologists.

At the ceremony, Minister Macklin said, 'It's an enormous privilege to be on your land, your country, on this significant occasion. The Wurundjeri people were the original custodians of this site and it is only fitting that it is now returned to them. This is an opportunity to better understand each other and it is days like today that makes it real.'

Above: Visitors explore Wil-im-ee Moor-ring at the handover ceremony, 23 October 2012.

Aboriginal children and houses at Coranderrk Aboriginal Station, c. 1870. Reproduced with permission from Museum Victoria (XP 2589).

CORANDERRK ABORIGINAL STATION AND CEMETERY

'Could we have our freedom to go away shearing and harvesting, and come home when we wish, and also to go for the good of our health when we need it; and we aboriginals all wish and hope to have freedom, not to be bound down by the protection of the board.' Petition from the people of Coranderrk, 22 September 1886.

In February 1859, Simon Wonga, the son of Billibellary, successfully petitioned Assistant Protector William Thomas to secure land for the Kulin at the Acheron and Goulburn rivers. After a year of planting and building fences, the government ordered them to relinquish their land to local pastoralists and move to another site that was highly unsuitable. In 1863, Wonga, supported by his cousin William Barak and preacher John Green, led forty people on a march over the mountain to a traditional site on Badgers Creek at Healesville. The ridge they crossed has since been known as the Black Spur.

This was the beginning of Coranderrk Aboriginal Station. They obtained the agreement of the government to reserve 2300 acres for farming and hunting. This was doubled in 1866, but halved in 1893. By the 1870s Coranderrk had a large village with a schoolhouse, bakery and butcher and a successful hop farm. Produce from Coranderrk won first prize at the Melbourne International Exhibition in 1872. Aboriginal handcrafted goods were sold to the many visitors to Coranderrk from Victoria and overseas.

For many years William Barak led an organised campaign by residents — including petitions and deputations to Melbourne — protesting their lack of rights and the threatened closure of the settlement by the Aborigines Protection Board. Despite initial successes, the station was undermined by government reversals in policy. The passing of the 'Half-caste' Act 1886 barred all Aboriginal people except so-called 'full bloods and half-castes aged under 14 or over 35' from Aboriginal reserves. The farm declined as a result and the land was progressively sold off to settlers. Nearby Healesville Sanctuary on Badgers Creek Road is located on former

William Barak's gravestone. Photograph by Peter Campbell.

act of Parliament. In 1998, the Indigenous Land Corporation assisted descendents of Coranderrk to purchase 0.81 acres of the land taken from their ancestors. Coranderrk remains extremely important to Victoria's Aboriginal people. The government of the time insisted that Koories adopt the village lifestyle and farming habits of Europeans yet when they were successful, they attracted the envy of landowners and were stripped of their country. However, important lessons were gained about the need for collective political action which mobilised later activists such as William Cooper.

In 2013, construction company Grocon announced plans to honour the memory of Barak with a 100-metre high vertical image on the facade of new building planned in Swanston Street, Melbourne.

Coranderrk has been written about by many historians, most recently by Giordano Nanni and Andrea James in their book, *Coranderrk: We Will Show the Country* (see Reference list, p. 138). The State Library of Victoria website also provides information and oral recordings about the impact of Coranderrk and other missions and reserves on Indigenous Victorians.

Coranderrk Aboriginal cemetery is part of the former Coranderrk Aboriginal Station at Healesville and contains approximately 300 burials of Aboriginal people including prominent leader and artist William Barak. It is five kilometres from the popular native wildlife park, Healesville Sanctuary.

Further information: The cemetery is on private land. Inquiries about access should be directed to the Wurundjeri Tribe Land Cultural Heritage Council.
Tel: (03) 8673 0901

Coranderrk land. Many residents were sent to Lake Tyers Mission, others to Maloga Mission and later to Cummeragunja Station in New South Wales.

Barak continued to live at Coranderrk until his death in 1903. An exhibition of his paintings was held at the National Gallery of Victoria in 1995. In 1924, Coranderrk was officially closed although one resident, Jemima Wandin Dunolly, remained there until she died in 1944. After the Second World War, the reservation on the remaining 1700 acres was cancelled and parcelled out for soldier resettlement. Aboriginal soldiers were not entitled to receive a grant of land.

In 1991, the half-acre cemetery with 300 burial places was returned to the Wurundjeri by an

WEST

Melbourne's west is one of the most diverse landscapes in Melbourne. It ranges from rural land in the far west to urban suburbs along the Maribyrnong River and Port Phillip Bay. It is a popular region for new immigrants with people from more than 130 different nations calling the area home.

The vast grasslands on the basalt plains attracted the interest of graziers from Tasmania. John Batman's expedition in 1835 disembarked from the *Rebecca* near today's Westgate Bridge to seek a treaty with the Kulin. Intensive industry began within fifteen years of settlement. From the 1920s many Aboriginal people arrived in the west seeking employment — some of whom became notable campaigners for social justice.

Archaeological evidence of Aboriginal occupation can be traced back to at least 30,000 years ago. Aboriginal people were living in the Maribyrnong Valley which was a temperate retreat in the last Ice Age. Most of the following sites lie along the Maribyrnong River once occupied near the coast by the Yalukit willam clan of the Boon Wurrung and further upriver by the Woiwurrung: the Marin balug clan on the western side and Wurundjeri clans on the eastern side. Bungarim, Ngurungaeta of the Marin balug, shared custodianship of the Mount William quarry (see p. 84).

Solomon's Ford. Photograph by Hari Ho.

SITES

WEST

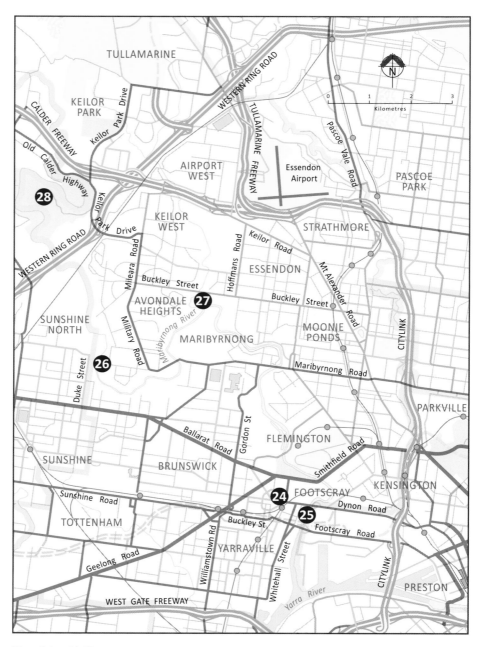

Map of sites 24–28.

William Cooper Bridge.

SITE 24
William Cooper Bridge

In 2010, the new Footscray railway station pedestrian bridge was named in honour of Aboriginal leader and activist William Cooper (1861–1941). Used by thousands of people every day, the bridge links the four platforms and buildings of the station to each other and the suburb. It was designed to engender a sense of place and identity. Its physical form makes reference to Footscray's industrial, commercial and social heritage.

In 1932, William Cooper was already 72 years of age when he arrived in Melbourne from Cummeragunja Station, New South Wales and began his remarkable campaign for social justice. Cooper revived the political strategies of marches, petitions and deputations used by the protesters at Coranderrk Aboriginal Station (see p. 87). He helped establish the Australian Aborigines' League along with Doug Nicholls, Marge Tucker, Geraldine Briggs, Ebenezer Lovett, Jack Patten, Bill and Eric Onus, Bruce Ferguson and others, using his home as its base. In 1938, they arranged a National Day of Mourning to mark Australia Day and the

DESCRIPTION
The William Cooper Bridge at Footscray railway station is named to commemorate a famous Footscray Aboriginal leader and campaigner for social justice.

LOCATION
Footscray railway station, corner of Hopkins and Irving Streets, Footscray.
Melway: 42 D5.

GETTING THERE
The Footscray railway station can be reached on the Sydenham rail line from Southern Cross and Flinders Stations.

TIME 20 minutes.

Street art painting near the east entrance to the William Cooper pedestrian rail bridge.

first deputation to the Prime Minister. Cooper, as secretary, also organised a petition to King George V seeking representation, enfranchisement and land rights. The Day of Mourning became known as Aborigines Day. In 1955, it was moved to the first Sunday in July where it became a day of celebration of Aboriginal culture, not just one of protest. Since then, it has evolved into NAIDOC Week (National Aborigines and Islanders Day Observance Committee). Aboriginal people across Australia were inspired by these initiatives to work collectively to affect change. Protesting their appalling conditions, several hundred people walked off the Cummeragunja Aboriginal Reserve on 4 February 1939 in the first mass strike of Aboriginal people in Australia.

Many regard Cooper as a founder of the Aboriginal civil rights movement which led to profound changes following the successful 1967 Referendum. The Referendum enabled Aboriginal people to be included in the census and empowered the Commonwealth to legislate on behalf of Aboriginal people living in the states.

On 6 October 2010, Cooper's memory was honoured when the Deputy Premier of Victoria opened the William Cooper Justice Centre which houses all three levels of Victorian Courts at the corner of William and Lonsdale Streets, Melbourne.

PROMINENT ABORIGINAL RESIDENTS FROM THE WESTERN SUBURBS FROM THE 1920–30s

Margaret (Marge) Tucker MBE lived in Pentland Parade, Seddon and worked in local industry in the 1920s. Tucker loved entertaining and was a great advocate for Aboriginal rights. She was the first Aboriginal women to serve on the Aboriginal Welfare Board. Her autobiography, *If Everyone Cared*, was very popular and created public awareness of the Stolen Generations. She was awarded the Order of the British Empire in 1968, recognising her service to the Aboriginal community.

Molly Dyer, Marge Tucker's daughter, lived with her mother in Seddon for a time. Mother of six children, she worked for the Aboriginal Advancement League and she was a founder of the Victorian Aboriginal Child Care Agency. She also provided foster care for nineteen children.

Sarah (Sally) Russell Cooper was William Cooper's daughter. She and her husband, Mick Russell, rented a house in Ballarat Rd, Footscray which became an unofficial boarding house for Aboriginal people and a place of social contact.

Lynch Cooper, William Cooper's son, was an early resident of Tarrengower Street, Yarraville. He was a well-known runner who won the 1928 Stawell Gift and the 1929 World Sprint at Olympic Park.

Connie Hart, a Gunditjmara woman who lived in Footscray, began weaving baskets in her 60s, recalling her early observations of her mother and local elders. She became a skilled artist and facilitated the regeneration of Victorian Aboriginal weaving practices.

Ebenezer Lovett was an activist for Aboriginal rights and the rights of the working class. He was a founder of the Aboriginal Advancement League.

Harold Blair, OAM was the first Aboriginal opera singer and played with Marge Tucker. He was also an Aboriginal activist. He joined the Aboriginal Advancement League and later the Federal Council for the Advancement of Aborigines and Torres Strait Islanders. He was an early member of the Aborigines Welfare Board. Blair was a teacher at two technical colleges then later at a conservatorium in Melbourne. In 1976, he was awarded the Order of Australia for his services to the arts and to the Aboriginal community.

Bill (Billy) Bargo was a well-known musician and rodeo rider from Queensland who was also a champion whip cracker. He lived in Ballarat Road, Footscray.

Alfred Turner, grandson of Aboriginal elder William Cooper. Photograph by Aaron Francis, courtesy Newspix.

THE JEWISH CONNECTION

William Cooper is a person revered by many from Melbourne's Jewish community. He had more than enough problems dealing with racial injustice against the Aboriginal community, yet it was a measure of the man that he found time to protest racism against other minorities. He organised the world's only private protest against Nazi Germany following the *Kristallnacht* pogrom against Jews in 1938. At 77 years of age, Cooper walked with a delegation from his Footscray home to the German consulate in Collins Street to lodge a protest petition.

Cooper has been honoured in Israel by the creation of an Academic Chair in his honour to support resistance and research of world holocaust studies. On 6 December 2012, Melbourne's Jewish community re-enacted the 1938 March from Cooper's home to Melbourne with members of Cooper's family to express their gratitude and their solidarity with the Indigenous cause.

Parkland at Grimes Reserve.

SITE 25
Grimes Reserve

Grimes Reserve is a park beside the Maribyrnong River in the historic waterside area of Footscray. On 21 March 1841, Aboriginal Chief Protector George Robinson, camped here after crossing the river on the Footscray punt from Melbourne on route to western Victoria. He wrote in his diary:

> …Camped for the night at the Salt Water River near the punt, west side. Saw native ovens as I rode along, some 12 feet wide; 4 (four) I saw in one place. It must have been a favourite resort.

The mounds once seen by Robinson indicate Grimes Reserve was a long-term and important willam for the Kulin. Mounds are often located beside rivers that were important travel and trade routes. They are usually the result of earth ovens where Koorie women cooked food by heating stones or burnt clay lumps in a pit. Meat and vegetables such as roots were placed on top of the heated rocks and the pit was sealed. After cooking, the debris was removed, eventually building up to sizeable mounds. The height of mounds could be an advantage near swampy waterways so sometimes huts

DESCRIPTION

Grimes Reserve beside the Maribyrnong River in Footscray was an important willam for the Kulin indicated by the many large Aboriginal mounds recorded there in 1841.

LOCATION

Grimes Reserve is bordered by Bunbury, Maribyrnong, Moreland Streets and the Maribyrnong River in Footscray. Melway: 42 E5.

GETTING THERE

Public transport: Catch a train to Footscray Station and walk down Bunbury Street from the station. Buses 216, 219, 220 or 402 pass in the area.

Car parking: Available in local streets.

Cycling/walking: The Maribyrnong River Trail connects north to Brimbank Park, south to Willamstown and east to the city centre.

TIME 20 minutes.

ACTIVITIES

The Footscray Art Centre with a cafe and facilities including public toilets is a few minutes walk north alongside the river and hosts a Koorie arts program including the annual Wominjeka Festival and Black Screen.

FURTHER INFORMATION

Tel: (03) 9362 8888
Web: www.footscrayarts.com

were built on them. At times, the mounds were also used for burials.

The large number of mounds at the reserve reflected the richness of fauna hunted by the Kulin clans in the grassy woodland and volcanic plains of Maribyrnong such as possums, the black wallaby, bush rat, eastern grey kangaroo, brown and yellow-footed antechinus and tuan.

Regular restocking of food supplies required the highly sophisticated use of fire on the native vegetation, especially when storage roots were underground in late summer before the autumn rains. Firing was done in patches to create a mosaic of areas at different stages of recovery. Fire-stick farming created forests and open plains where edible plants could grow and grazing animals like kangaroos could thrive.

Local history records indicate that Aboriginal people also camped at Footscray Park north of the reserve with large kangaroo dogs beside a creek which provided them with plentiful eels. This creek would have been the forerunner of today's ornamental ponds.

Grimes Reserve was known as Batman Reserve from 1943 until the 1970s as it was believed John Batman landed there during his expedition in 1835 to sign a treaty with Kulin leaders. Aboriginal people performed in Grimes Reserve to contribute to centenary celebrations of Victoria which were held there in 1937. Activist William Cooper formally protested afterwards that the civic speeches made no mention at all of Aboriginal people.

Solomon's Ford, location of the fish trap in 1803. Photograph by Hari Ho.

SITE 26
Solomon's Ford fish trap

Fish were an important source of food to local Aboriginal people and a large amount of ingenuity was used to capture them. The first European visitor to record a working fish trap in Victoria was Charles Grimes, the Surveyor-General of New South Wales. His expedition to Port Phillip Bay in 1803 recorded an Aboriginal fish trap at Solomon's Ford near what is today Avondale Heights. The many basalt rocks scattered in the water in the area of Solomon's Ford today may have been used in the fish trap construction. A scarred tree and quarry site recorded in the vicinity indicate it was an important Kulin willam. The ford also marked the tidal limit of salt water: it provided both fresh water and a key crossing point for Aboriginal people and later early settlers.

Eels were a staple of the Kulin diet and were harvested in large numbers during their migrations to and from the sea. In early spring, young eels (elvers) travel upstream. During autumn, mature eels aged up to 15–35 years or more migrate to the bay on a long journey to reach breeding grounds in the tropical ocean. Traps were often set in streams where the water flow was shallow or the stream narrowed. A weir made

DESCRIPTION

A shallow ford in the Maribyrnong Valley was the first recorded location of an Aboriginal fish trap in Melbourne and an important crossing place on the river.

LOCATION

Canning Street, Avondale Heights. Melway: 27 B8.

GETTING THERE

A walking trail leads downhill from Burke Street, Braybrook (Melway: 27 B9) to the ford on the river. Alternatively, the east side of the river can be accessed from Canning Street.

Car parking: Burke and Duke Streets. Melway: 27 B9.

Public transport: Bus number 220 from Queens Street, Melbourne. Walk from Western Highway (Ballarat Road) to Duke Street.

Cycling/walking: The Maribyrnong River Trail runs for twenty-eight kilometres from Southbank in the city all the way to Brimbank Park in the North West. The full track can be cycled in three hours.

TIME 45 minutes.

Maribrynong River. Photograph by Hari Ho.

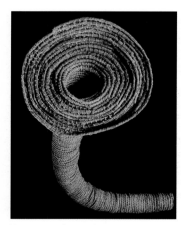

Victorian eel trap. Courtesy Museum of South Australia.

of basalt boulders or woven rushes could be constructed across the stream. Some weirs were straight; some were curved; while others had wings which directed the fish to the centre. Holes in the weirs would allow the fish to pass through into funnel-shaped fishing pots made of woven plant fibres. Captured eels could be killed with a bite to the back of the head then strung on sticks, or placed in water-filled pits and cooked later. Other fishing methods included using lit torches to attract fish to the surface where they were speared, or by dragging stream beds with a bag net (see also Site 11, p. 37).

Lily Street lookout.

SITE 27
Lily Street lookout and quarry

The Lily Street lookout on the rim of the ancient Maribyrnong Valley provides one of Melbourne's most spectacular views. On the plain below can be seen the junction of Steele Creek and the Maribyrnong River. To the west are the distant towers of Melbourne. A few metres below the lookout and to the right can also be seen a large outcrop of silcrete boulders protruding from the slopes which bear marks from quarrying by Koories.

The Lily Street quarry is one of many Aboriginal silcrete quarries and working sites along the length of the Maribyrnong River valley and its tributaries. Over 2300 Aboriginal camp sites have been found in the Kulin lands around Melbourne and most were discovered through scatters of flaked stone resulting from men chipping to make tools. Silcrete was the most widely used stone and is found at most archaeological sites on the Western Plains. Deposits usually result from the weathering of basalt into the ground water below. Grey is a

DESCRIPTION

A silcrete stone quarry site used by Aboriginal people can be viewed from the spectacular Lily Street lookout in the Maribyrnong Valley.

LOCATION

Lily Street, Essendon West. Melway: 27 J4.

GETTING THERE

From the end of Lily Street, off Buckley Street in Essendon West, a walking trail leads 70 metres to the Lily Street lookout. From there follow the Maribyrnong River Trail downhill.

Thirty metres downhill and five metres to the left of the trail is the silcrete site of large boulders.

Public transport: From Essendon Station on the Broadmeadows line take bus number 465 to Lily Street. Transport information inquiries: 1800 800 007.

Car parking: Available via the gravel drive at the end of Lily Street.

Cycling/walking: The Maribyrnong River Trail from Lily Street runs 8 kilometres west to Brimbank Park, and south to Footscray.

SITE 27

WEST

TIME 30–45 minutes.

OTHER ACTIVITIES

The lookout offers magnificent views of the Maribyrnong River Valley. The site is on the Maribyrnong River Heritage Trail which provides information on historic places.

FURTHER INFORMATION

Parks Victoria
Tel: 13 19 63 or
Web: www.parkweb.vic.gov.au

CONSIDERATIONS

Care should be taken to keep to the official paths for safety and to avoid erosion to the hillside.

common colour at silcrete sites but yellow, brown, red, green and orange also occur.

Two large silcrete boulders also showing marks from Aboriginal toolmaking are located at the entrance of an historic cave beside Steele Creek (north side) near its junction with the Maribyrnong River at the base of the lookout.

Silcrete boulders near the Lily Street lookout show evidence of chipping to manufacture stone tools.

Ford at Brimbank Park.

SITE 28
Kulin Wetlands

Brimbank Park in the Maribyrnong Valley is one of the oldest sites of human occupation in Australia. This beautiful park is encircled by a bend of the Maribyrnong River and sheltered by the towering 'brim' of the Maribyrnong Valley. The valley provided a temperate retreat for humans during and after the Ice Age which ended 10,000 years ago.

Archaeological sites that show evidence of Aboriginal people's activities in Brimbank Park include scarred trees, burials, stone quarries, axes, scatters of stone tools, bone remnants, ochre, charcoal and hearth stones, blades and scrapers. Further discoveries are still being made. In 2008, a 15,000-year-old hearth (fireplace) was uncovered in the park during building excavations. Park staff maintain a close working relationship with the Wurundjeri people in the cultural management of the Maribyrnong Valley.

In 1940, a human skull and femur were found during quarrying, upriver from Brimbank Park near the junction of the Maribyrnong River and Dry Creek. This discovery had a dramatic impact on our understanding of Aboriginal history

DESCRIPTION

Brimbank Park, the western suburbs' largest park, is one of Australia's oldest human occupation areas including the Kulin Wetlands site dated back to 17,000 years.

LOCATION

The wetlands can be reached via a rock ford on the Maribyrnong River except when the river is running high. A circular track leads around the former quarry site at the river's junction with Taylor Creek. Directions to the wetlands are available from the visitors centre near the car park. Melway: 14 G9.

GETTING THERE

Vehicle access is via Brimbank Road off Keilor Park Drive. Melway: 15 B10.

Public transport: Train to Essendon, on the Broadmeadows line, then the Taylors Lakes bus to Keilor.

Cycling/walking: The Maribyrnong Trail runs from Brimbank Park to Melbourne (22 kilometres).

FACILITIES

Visitors centre, picnic and barbecue sites, public toilets, walking trails and views. Platypuses inhabit this area of the river.

TIME 60–90 minutes.

FURTHER INFORMATION

Parks Victoria
Tel: 13 19 63 or
Web: www.parkweb.vic.gov.au

Sieving earth at the Keilor archaeological excavation. Courtesy Aboriginal Affairs Victoria.

in Australia. 'Keilor Man' has been estimated to be 14,500 years old, which at that time, was the earliest evidence of humans in the country. Further excavation uncovered one of most complete records of occupation in Australia dating back 30,000 years. About 2000 items of worked stone were located up to seven metres deep. These included ancient basalt cobbles to more recent microliths (small flints). Bone remains of extinct creatures such as giant kangaroos and wombats, diprotodonts and marsupial lions were also unearthed.

In 1965, the remains of a man and woman, approximately 6500 years old, were found downstream at Green Gully in Brimbank Park during quarrying near the junction of the Maribyrnong River and Taylors Creek. Analysis of tools and charcoals indicate occupation by humans up to 17,000 years ago. The site was purchased by the Victorian government and is now known as the Kulin Wetlands.

The Green Gully and Keilor remains have since been returned to country and reburied with traditional rites by the Wurundjeri people.

SOUTH

The southern region of Melbourne is dominated by Port Phillip Bay. The winding urban coastline south of the city is one of the most popular stretches of foreshore in Australia, beloved by Melbournians for its spectacular views, bushland, beaches and walking and cycling paths.

Prior to colonisation, the Boon Wurrung people were custodians of this area which was abundant in food and rich in spiritual significance. This coastline is a songline (Dreaming track) along which the Boon Wurrung camped during their annual seasonal travels as evidenced by ancient middens, wells, ochre and ceremonial sites.

Songlines are the paths across the land or skies that mark the routes of creation beings during the Dreaming.

View from Beach Road looking towards Red Bluff. Photograph by Hari Ho.

SITES

Of interest: Boon Wurrung Foundation

30. Point Ormond Hill lookout

31. Bayside Coastal Indigenous Trail

32. Mordialloc Aboriginal Reserve

SOUTH

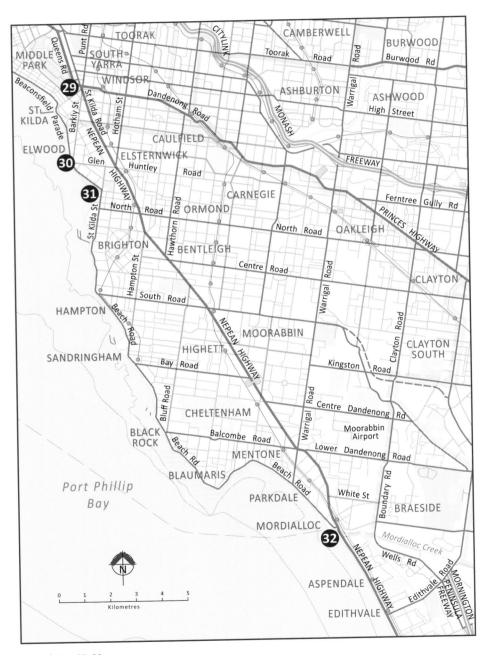

Map of sites 29–32.

A Corroboree on Emerald Hill in 1840, 1875, W Liardet, Watercolour with pen and ink, gouache and pencil. State Library of Victoria, H28250/31.

BOON WURRUNG FOUNDATION

When early settler ships arrived in Hobsons Bay on route to the Yarra, one of the first landmarks they saw was a strikingly green hill surrounded by lagoons near the foreshore. It was named Emerald Hill by journalist Edmund Finn who recalled:

> It was at all times a favourite trysting-place of the blacks, who held corroborees and native dances there, a pantomimic performance occasionally witnessed by Melbournians on fine summer nights…This once beautiful eminence…was the grazing ground of the kangaroo until a sheep station and the strange-looking animals that accompanied it scared them away.

In Kulin society, these prominences were often sites for social exchange, trade and ceremonies. In the new British colony such high points were favoured for civic and religious buildings. The former South Melbourne Town Hall building replaced the Boon Wurrung willam on Emerald Hill in 1880.

The Nerre Nerre Minnim area (South Melbourne) was in the estate of the Yalukit willam clan of the Boon Wurrung. A favoured camp was at nearby Albert Park Lake where their miams were often seen. In July 1844 they camped at Nerre Nerre Minnim with Wathaurong allies after arriving in Melbourne for cultural business.

In 1840, settlers were invited to witness a Ngargee at Emerald Hill to experience Aboriginal culture. Artist Wilbraham Liardet, the founder of Port Melbourne, later painted the event. Poet Richard Howitt described the fifty men performing tightly choreographed dances with the musical accompaniment of women as a sight to, 'haunt the soul for years after such exhibitions. You hear the wild songs, see the dusky moving figures.'

Traditional owners have returned to Emerald Hill in the form of the Boon Wurrung Foundation, now located in the former South Melbourne Town Hall building in Bank Street. The Foundation provides consultancy, training and advice to government, Indigenous and community groups, corporate and non-government organisations and educational institutions.

Foundation director Carolyn Briggs is a well-known spokesperson who has addressed the Parliament of Victoria and is regularly invited to deliver the 'welcome to country' address at public events.

Stories of the kidnapping of Carolyn Briggs, great-grandmother of Louisa Briggs, and the Boon Wurrung 'time of chaos' can be found on the Bayside Coastal Indigenous Trail (see Site 31, p. 115).

Further information: Tel: (03) 9682 9578; Web: www.boonwurrung.org.

Ngargee tree plaque.

St Kilda Ngargee tree near the corner of Queens Road and Fitzroy Street.

DESCRIPTION

An ancient red gum tree in Albert Park near St Kilda Junction is recorded as an Aboriginal Ngargee (corroboree) site and continues today as a venue for many reconciliation activities. Native grasslands and a ceremonial circle are nearby.

LOCATION

The tree is located in Albert Park on the corner of Fitzroy Street and Queens Road, St Kilda. Melway: 58 B7.

GETTING THERE

From the corner of Fitzroy Street and St Kilda Road, walk north in the parkland for 120 metres till you reach the only large red gum tree.

SITE 29
St Kilda Ngargee tree

The Ngargee tree in Albert Park near the northeast end of Fitzroy Street is estimated to be 300–500 years old. The tree is the last survivor of a thick wattle forest interspersed with mature gums. Nearby St Kilda Junction is the historic meeting point of tracks to the southern, northern and eastern districts. Assistant Protector William Thomas noted that the Boon Wurrung clans frequently camped in this area. For example, in November 1847 and February and September 1848, they were camping near Fitzroy Street.

Albert Park Lake, located a few hundred metres away, was an important willam for the Yalukit willam clan of the Boon Wurrung. They were seen hunting and gathering and building bark shelters beside the lagoon which teemed with gunabi (ducks) and gunuwarra (swans). Starch could be extracted from roots of plants in the lagoon to make damper. Wildlife such as tortoises, eels, frogs, fish, and freshwater shellfish were harvested. Four or five hours of foraging each day was usually sufficient to meet family needs.

According to Assistant Protector William Thomas, the Boon Wurrung held meetings every three months and corroborees were held at full and new moons. Notices were distributed to neighbours via message sticks and smoke signals, and during these inter-tribal gatherings marriages were arranged, and disputes settled.

St Kilda was known as Euro-yuroke meaning the grinding stone site. This referred to the sandstone at the St Kilda Esplanade used by men to sharpen their stone axes. According to a Kulin Dreaming story, the ancestral creator Bunjil placed rocks at the north end of the bay to stop the great flood. These sacred rocks may refer to today's prominences such as St Kilda Hill, Ormond Hill, Emerald Hill or the Esplanade bluff.

The Ngargee tree is an object of affection and reverence by many St Kilda residents. Since the 1950s, locals have intervened on several occasions to save the tree from harm. More recently, it has been a focus for many reconciliation projects. A native bushland, billabong and extensive native grasslands with wallaby and kangaroo grass have been created around it. A ceremonial dance circle and artworks have also been built nearby as a focus for reconciliation and cultural activities.

Public transport: Tram 16 from Swanston Walk, City of Melbourne.

Car parking: Available in Fitzroy Street.

Cycling/walking: The tree is ten minutes walk from the Bay Trail.

TIME 30–45 minutes.

OTHER ACTIVITIES

Albert Park is one of Victoria's most visited parks. Nearby are Luna Park, St Kilda Beach, many cafes and restaurants in Fitzroy Street and Acland Street.

FURTHER INFORMATION

A self-guided walk, the Yalukit Willam Trail leads from the tree to the foreshore. It is available in the publication 'Walks in Port Phillip' or from City of Phillip libraries and town halls. City of Port Phillip
Tel: (03) 9209 6777
Web: www.portphillip.vic. gov.au
Email: walking@portphillip.vic. gov.au

WILLAMS (MEETING PLACES)

Fawkner Park (Melway: 2L D6) on Commercial Road, South Yarra and the land north of the park as far as the Yarra River comprised one of several Aboriginal reserves created by the government as protected areas due to the pressure of European settlement. However, Fawkner Park was only one of the regular places used by the clans around South Yarra. Others documented by the City of Stonnington in consultation with traditional owners include:

1. Bushland between the park and the nearby Church of England Grammar School in Domain Road

3. Royal Botanical Gardens

4. Government House

5. Melbourne High School playing field, formerly banks of swamp at Yarra Street alongside the South Yarra Railway Bridge where Derrimut camped

6. Williams Road in the late 1840–50s

7. Lake Como in Como Park near Williams Road in the late 1840–50s

8. Toorak Hotel where 'Murrey, the king of the Yarra Yarra tribe' camped

9. Junction of Toorak Road and Chapel Street where the Kurnai visiting from Gippsland camped in the gully and tea-tree scrub

10. Chapel Street, between Commercial Road and Dandenong Road

11. Mount Erica Hotel near the corner of High Street and Williams Road

12. High Street, near Malvern Town Hall

13. South Yarra Railway Bridge along Yarra Street

14. South Yarra Depot, near Clara Street — campsite of Derrimut. Beruke (also called Gellibrand), a well-known member of the Native Police Corps, was buried in the area on 4 January 1852

15. Southeast corner of Punt and Commercial Roads where the Kulin met to celebrate the marriage of the Prince of Wales in 1863

16. Kooyong Park, Malvern where approximately 1500 artefacts were excavated in the 1970s (see p. 46)

17. Le Mans Swamp, now Caulfield Park.

In the *Prahran Telegraph* of 16 October 1896, Joseph Crook recalled Aboriginal gatherings in Fawkner Park near today's Tennis Centre opposite Hope Street (Melway: 2L B5):

> The only amusement we had up to 1851 was the natives used to meet once a month on the full moon in Fawkner Park, opposite the Fawkner Hotel there was no hotel, park or streets there then, but all bush. There the blacks held their corroboree, and I have seen the greater portion of the people of Melbourne and Prahran turn out and visit the camp on those occasions. We thought it grand fun and so did the natives, for while the dance was going on some of the old men used to go among the visitors with an old hat, and collect money, from the proceeds…

For further information, visit the Indigenous history section of the City of Stonnington's website: www.stonnington.vic.gov.au.

Point Ormand Hill lookout.

SITE 30
Point Ormond Hill lookout

From the top of Point Ormond Hill in Elwood is a superb view of St Kilda, Hobsons Bay and the distant towers of Melbourne's city centre. The marine reef offshore as well as the nearby wetland (today Elwood Canal) made the Point an important food gathering site for the Boon Wurrung people.

In the autumn of 1840 Aboriginal women were visiting Point Ormond three times a week to collect shellfish. John Butler Cooper's book, *History of St Kilda 1840–1930*, says that, 'Aboriginals came to the Red Bluff (Point Ormond), the sands thereabouts containing large beds of cockles.... Mounds of shells once to be seen on the beach at Elwood and St Kilda told the tale of Aboriginal shellfish feasts…' In 1974, stone axes were retrieved from a Boon Wurrung shell midden uncovered during roadworks.

Today the hill is just a remnant of what was once a curving cliff called Little Red Bluff which provided a strategic lookout. Other clans could be located by the smoke rising from their campfires on the horizon and they could scout for game such as kangaroo or emu. High places also offer a defensive

DESCRIPTION
Aboriginal people camped at Point Ormond Hill in Elwood and regularly harvested shellfish. They were expelled in 1840 when the site became Victoria's first quarantine station and St Kilda's first cemetery.

LOCATION
Point Ormond Hill is west of the junction of Glenhuntly Road and Marine Parade, St Kilda. Melway: 67 A2–3.

GETTING THERE
Public transport: Elsternwick Station and then bus number 246 to Marine Parade, Elwood.

Cycling/walking: Point Ormond is located beside the Bay Trail running north to Port Melbourne and south to Brighton.

Car parking: Available at the end of Point Ormond Road.

TIME 30 minutes.

location against attack. The dunes behind the hill provided shelter from ocean weather. The red and yellow sandstone at the bluff may have also been a source of ochre for paint and performance.

On 17 April 1940, the *Glen Huntley* bounty ship, overcrowded with Scottish immigrants, docked in the bay flying the yellow fever flag. It was ordered to remove its crew and passengers to a quarantine station urgently set up at Point Ormond under guard by soldiers. Three passengers eventually died and were buried on the crown of the hill. On 19 April 1840, Superintendent Charles La Trobe ordered Assistant Protector William Thomas to expel all Aboriginal encampments from Melbourne because the disease-ridden ship was located near where the Aboriginal women collected mussels. Thomas said he could not convince the women that La Trobe's intentions were humane as they argued 'white men only would die'.

The last census of the Boon Wurrung, taken in 1863, recorded only eleven individuals from a population estimated to be 250–500 prior to settlement. European diseases were an important factor in the drastic reduction of the Kulin population. In May 1839, Aboriginal encampments on the Yarra were assessed by the settlement's medical officer as being disastrously affected by syphilis, typhus, bronchial disease, dysentery and tuberculosis. There is evidence that even before Melbourne's settlement, half the Kulin may have died in each of two epidemics of smallpox that spread overland from settlers and traders in 1790 and 1830.

SITE 31
Bayside Coastal Indigenous Trail

The fifteen locations of the Trail (part of the larger Bayside Coastal Trail) were chosen to show the direct relationship between Aboriginal people and their history, social customs and environment. Several sites are based on stories by Boon Wurrung elder, Carolyn Briggs, and feature contemporary Aboriginal art and sculptures by artists Ellen Jose, Glenn Romanis, Pauline Reynolds, Vicki Couzens, and Bindi Cole. The sites are connected by seventeen kilometres of bicycle and walking paths that extend from Elwood to Beaumaris. Melbourne's largest marine sanctuary is near the south end of the trail where rock pools reveal the rich marine fauna and flora which were harvested before settlement.

Many of Australia's most celebrated sculptors and painters have also been inspired by the spiritual and aesthetic power of Bayside's coastline and their works are included in an additional seventy-five trail markers featuring themes of art, history, architecture and environment.

The fifteen markers are listed in the order they appear along the shoreline, starting at the northern most point, Elwood. There are four intersecting trails so they do not appear in numerical order.

DESCRIPTION

The Bayside Indigenous Heritage Trail features fifteen panels, artworks and installations over 17 kilometres of spectacular urban coastline that provide insight into the culture and history of the Boon Wurrung people.

LOCATION

From Elwood Beach (Melway: 67 C5) to Moysey Gardens, Keys and Beach Road, Beaumaris (Melway: 86 E9).

GETTING THERE

Car: Vehicles can visit trail locations via Beach Road which follows the coastline from Elwood to Beaumaris.

Cycling/walking: Markers and three sculptures are located on the continuous bicycle and walking tracks on the coastline starting from Elwood Beach (opposite Head Street) to Moysey Gardens (opposite Keys Road, Beaumaris).

Above: Bayside coastline, north of Red Bluff.

SOUTH

Public toilets are on the trail as well as car parks, marinas, cafes, swimming beaches and marine clubs. Bayside Mobility Maps indicating accessible parking, toilets, seating and transport are available from the web or from Bayside Council. A free smart phone app with audio-tours of walks and trails can also be downloaded from the Bayside Council website (see below).

TIME Half day

FURTHER INFORMATION

Bayside City Council
Tel: (03) 9599 4444
Web: www.bayside.vic.gov.au

Marine Care Ricketts Point
Web: www.marinecare.org.au/index.php/sanctuary/aboriginal

OTHER ACTIVITIES

The Bayside Coastal Trail features ninety panels and signs on different themes including Indigenous, art, history, architecture and environment.

Above: Middle Brighton Pier. Photograph by Hari Ho.

Suggested route

Last Arweets

In the first years after settlement, there were two Arweets (clan leaders) of the Boon Wurrung — Derrimut (see Site 19, p. 70) and Benbow (panel 5). **Location:** Elwood Beach opposite Head Street, Melway: 67 C5.

The barraimal

This marker tells the story of the old man barraimal (emu) who had to take over the role of the female barraimal and look after the eggs (panel 12). **Location:** Middle Brighton Pier. Melway: 67 B10.

The barraimal constellation

A sculpture depicting the barraimal constellation created by the Southern Cross, Pointer, Scorpio, Sagittarius and Coalsack Nebula to create the body, nest and eggs (panel 13). **Location:** Middle Brighton Pier. Melway: 67 B10.

Journey of the eel

February and March were the months of the wygabil-ny-ewin (eel season) when female eels begin their long journey down the Birrarung (Yarra) River to Nairm (Port Phillip Bay). The

Dendy Street Beach. Photograph by Hari Ho.

return of the eels in Pareip (spring) was celebrated through dances and celebrations (panel 2). **Location**: Middle Brighton Pier. Melway: 67 B10.

Boon Wurrung women

For many thousands of years the Boon Wurrung women journeyed to their meeting places along the coastal area of Bayside connecting to country, the great spirits of Bunjil the eagle and Waarn (Waa) the crow (panel 3).

Dendy Street Beach is also the site of inner Melbourne's largest Aboriginal midden. It was a popular fishing site where clans camped and cooked shellfish and other foods for up to two thousand years or more. (See also Dendy Street midden p. 114.) **Location**: Dendy Street Beach, Brighton. Melway: 76 C1.

Boon Wurrung people of the peninsula

The Boon Wurrung was an extended language-based family group, consisting of six clans: Yalukit willam, Ngaruk willam, Mayune balug, Boonwurrung balug, Yownegerra and the Yallock balluk (panel 4). **Location**: Green Point, Brighton. Melway: 76 C3.

DENDY STREET BEACH MIDDEN

The largest midden in inner Melbourne, the Dendy Street Beach midden is one kilometre long and is located within the natural dune system behind the public beachfront. More than 350 middens have been recorded around Port Phillip Bay.

Middens are former cooking fires with layers of shells and charcoal that remain from Aboriginal meals. They may also contain fish and animal bones, burnt stones and tools. They appear as layers of shell exposed in the sides of dunes, banks or cliff tops or as scatters of shell on eroded surfaces. Their size can range from a few metres to hundreds of metres across and from a thin single layer to multiple layers.

Brighton was one of the most popular fishing places for the Boon Wurrung in Melbourne before two miles (3.2 kilometres) of the Brighton foreshore was sold to Henry Dendy in 1841. Dendy Street Beach was an ideal willam. Sand dunes provided shelter from the wind and sun and a soft place for sitting. Native trees provided firewood and shelters. Most

importantly, there is a very large shallow reef adjoining the beach. Reefs are good sources of shellfish and crustaceans. These in turn attract fish which could be speared. Stone traps could be built on reefs using the tide to strand fish. Stone from the reef could be used to sharpen tools or provide rocks to increase the heat of fires.

At Brighton, Kulin women in particular harvested shellfish and many of the plants found on the coast such as Karawun (Mat Rush), Kummeree (Pigface), Worike (Banksia), Bowat (Poa Grass), Kabin (Running Postman) and Seaberry.

When the midden was first analysed in 1967, it had three different shell and charcoal layers: 51cm (20 inches), 2.5cm (1 inch) and 20cm (8 inches) thick respectively. These layers indicate different intensities of occupation in the area's history. About seven different kinds of edible shellfish are typically found in Melbourne's middens such as mussels, oysters, warreners, pipis, abalone, limpets, turbos and whelks. Today the Brighton midden is mostly concealed by plants which prevent erosion.

Considerations: Observe all fence security and signs. All Aboriginal cultural places and their artefacts in Victoria are protected by law.

Above left: Dendy Street Beach. Above right: Shells and charcoal from Aboriginal cooking fires.

View from Beach Road looking towards Red Bluff. Photograph by Hari Ho.

Natural resources of the Boon Wurrung

The Bayside region was rich in natural resources and supported the Boonwurrung balug clan and visiting wurrungs (language groups) who travelled to the area as part of the annual journey cycle (panel 6). **Location**: Picnic Point, Sandringham. Melway: 76 E8.

Boon Wurrung landscapes

The country around what is today known as the Peninsula was very different 200 years ago. For the Boon Wurrung, the landscape of their country included swamps, lagoons, rivers, open grassy country and thinly timbered country (panel 1). **Location**: Beach Road opposite Sims Street, Sandringham. Melway: 76 G10.

Time of chaos

This panel tells the story of when the Boon Wurrung was in conflict with other Kulin nations and neglected their land (panel 9). **Location**: Beach Road opposite Sims Street. Sandringham. Melway: 76 G10.

Bunjil's Eggs sculpture by Ray Thomas. Photograph by Hari Ho.

The Bullarto N'yoweenth (plenty of sun) season

Shell middens are a record of when the Boon Wurrung women and visiting neighbours harvested shell fish and fish every year from November to February (panel 7). **Location**: Beach Road, north of Royal Avenue, Sandringham. Melway: 76 H11.

The Ancient Yarra River with Bunjil's eggs

This sculpture references the ancient channels of the Yarra and Werribee rivers on the floor of the Bay 10,000 years ago with the eggs representing six traditional groups of the Boon Wurrung people (panel 14). (See also Lost Country, facing page.)

Nearby, freshwater springs, once used by the Boon Wurrung, seep through the dunes onto the sandstone rock platform at the back of the beach at the north end of Half Moon Bay, just before Red Bluff and gather in rock holes. Three holes in the rock bordering the dune have been widened into wells. **Location**: Cliff top from Red Bluff car park, opposite Eliza Street, Sandringham. Melway: 85 H1.

Louisa Briggs: living across two worlds

Born in 1830s, Louisa Briggs, the great-grandmother of Boon Wurrung elder Carolyn Briggs, was kidnapped with other women from the Bayside area by sealers and taken to islands in Bass Strait but returned to Melbourne in 1852 (panel 8). **Location**: Black Rock Yacht Club. Melway: 85 H2.

Ochre pits

The ochre pits of Bayside provided the Boon Wurrung with a palate for art for use in dance, performance, ceremonies and Ngargee (panel 11). (See also Ochre site, Black Rock Gardens, p. 119.) **Location**: Car park, Beach Road, south of Balcombe Road. Sandringham. Melway: 85 K5.

LOST COUNTRY, THE GREAT FLOOD

A former Aboriginal willam including a lookout and midden is perched high on the cliff above Black Rock beach and Marina (Melway: 85 H3). From here, there is an extraordinary view across Port Phillip Bay and the lands of the Boon Wurrung. Mount Martha can be seen to the south, the You Yangs and Bellarine Peninsula to the west and Mount Macedon to the north. Directly below is the reef which provided the food collected in all weathers by Kulin women for cooking at the midden behind the lookout. Across the waters, ships can be seen on the sea road or channel.

Scientists believe that Port Phillip Bay was dry land during the last Ice Age when this view would have been of a vast plain where the ancestors of the Boon Wurrung people hunted and gathered. During this era they could have walked to Hobart, Tasmania. When the Ice Age ended, temperatures began to rise, causing great ice sheets to melt and sea levels to increase world-wide by several metres. New Guinea and Tasmania were separated from the continent and about 12,000 years ago the sea reached what are now the Port Phillip Heads and began to flow into Port Phillip Bay, covering low-lying land, reaching as far inland as today's suburb of Flemington. About 3000 years ago the bay entrance may have been blocked by sand and silt. The Bay again returned to dry land leaving a relatively small lake fed by the Yarra and Werribee Rivers. Perhaps a thousand years ago the Bay entrance unblocked and flooded again. This may have happened rapidly with the catastrophic effects described in Aboriginal accounts.

Melbourne's Kulin have an oral tradition describing the flooding of Port Phillip Bay

Lookout (south of upper carpark, Black Rock Marina).

where their ancestors once hunted on dry land across which the Yarra flowed. The flooding of the Bay has also been offered as an explanation as to why the Boon Wurrung people have a coastal territory: the rising seas may have forced them off the flooding plains to the edges of other tribal lands.

Early settler Georgina McCrae wrote in her journal:

> Robert Russell says that Mr Cobb talks to the blacks in their own language and the following is an account given by them, of the formation of Port Phillip Bay: "Plenty long ago…gago, gego, gugo… alonga Corio, men could cross, dryfoot, from our side of the Bay to Geelong." They described a hurricane — trees bending to and fro — then the earth sank, and the sea rushed in through the Heads, till the void places became broad and deep, as they are today.

The installation of bluestone and yellow ochre sandstone representing the six clans of the Boon Wurrung. Photograph by Hari Ho.
Right: Ricketts Point well site.

Boon Wurrung blossom

The installation of bluestone and yellow ochre sandstone north of Rickets Point Tea House represents the six clans of the Boon Wurrung (panel 15). Melway: 86 B8.

Ricketts Point is also the location of Melbourne's most historic Aboriginal freshwater well. It is located on the beach at the foot of the dunes, forty metres north of the Beaumaris Yacht Club, but today it is usually buried by sand. It was fed by springs that flow from the dune at the back of the beach. A channel carved in the rock assisted the flow. According to Aldo Massola, the former Curator of Anthropology at Museum Victoria, the mouth of the well was originally narrower so it could be covered by bark or stone by Aboriginal people to keep the water clean. Later it may have been widened by shepherds, fisherman and visitors to immerse a billy. Inflow of water to this well was once measured at four gallons (18 litres) per hour, enough for a small group or family. **Location**: Ricketts Point Sanctuary, north of Reserve Road, Beaumaris. Melway: 86 B8.

The time of change

In the late 1700s the Boon Wurrung made their first sightings of white people in ships. In 1803 they observed the first European settlement near Sorrento (panel 10). **Location**: Moysey Garden, Beach Road opposite Keys Road, Beaumaris. Melway: 86 E9.

OCHRE SITE, BLACK ROCK GARDENS

The ochre pits provide a direct link to the culture and history of the Boon Wurrung people. The pits provided them with a palate for art, especially for live body art used in dance and performance, ceremonial customs and celebrations. Ochre was gathered from certain multi-coloured bluffs protruding onto the beaches at Black Rock, Sandringham and Beaumaris. This soft iron-rich sand provides hues of red, yellow, brown and orange. It could be crushed in the many depressions or pits in the horizontal rock slabs that run from the base of the cliffs to the sea.

For the Boon Wurrung clans, ochre is an important part of maintaining customs and oral history as well as providing a focus for entertainment and enjoyment. Early European settlers sometimes attended these spectacular and highly choreographed events. The dance is usually conducted at night, backed by a large bonfire to illuminate the performance and to provide an exciting atmosphere, the men using ochre to paint circle patterns around their eyes. As the flames sparked from the green eucalyptus leaves, the drumming of the women intensified, the rhythm beat faster and the pace of the men intensified.

Ochre cliffs on foreshore below Black Rock Gardens (Melway: 85 K5).

Attenborough Park is located within the former Mordialloc Aboriginal Reserve and ration depot beside the Mordialloc Creek. In the Peter Scullin Reserve adjacent to Beach Road opposite Centreway (Melway: 92 E1) is a memorial plaque commemorating the Aboriginal people of the area and the founding settler who distributed rations.

LOCATION

Nepean Highway, Aspendale. The park is on the south side of Mordialloc Creek near the coast. Melway: 92 G2.

GETTING THERE

Public transport: Mordialloc rail station is approximately one kilometre from Attenborough Park.

Car parking: Parking is available in Scullin Reserve and Attenborough Park.

Above: Attenborough Park by the Mordialloc Creek. Photograph by Hari Ho.

SITE 32
Mordialloc Aboriginal Reserve

The suburb of Mordialloc lies on the foreshore of Port Phillip Bay where the Mordialloc Creek meets the sea. Its name derives from the Kulin term 'Mordy Yallock', meaning 'near little sea'. The sand dunes here were a favourite summer willam for the Boon Wurrung people, who harvested eels, small marsupials and water fowl from the creek and swamps and collected shellfish along the shore during their annual travels. The creek lay at the north end of the vast Karrum Karrum (Carrum) swamp which extended fifteen kilometres south and was a rich Kulin hunting ground.

An Aboriginal reserve was set aside for the Boon Wurrung in 1852. It was one of several reserves created by the government which was keen to move the clans away from the central city. Mordialloc Aboriginal Reserve comprised of 832 acres on both sides of Mordialloc Creek with the main Aboriginal camp on the south side in today's Attenborough Park. Alexander MacDonald, one of the earliest settlers, distributed government rations to the community from a depot.

Jimmy and Nancy Dunbar, residents of the Mordialloc reserve. Left: Sitting outside the Bridge Hotel, c. 1870s.

FACILITIES

The well-appointed recreation area is close to Mordialloc Pier with tennis court, fishing, kiosk, toilets and barbecue. Bike and walking trails extends north and south along the foreshore and inland along Mordialloc Creek. Scullin Reserve has a playground, toilets and restaurant.

The Bridge Hotel still exists today and is open for lunch and dinner.

TIME 45–60 minutes.

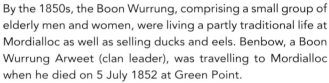

By the 1850s, the Boon Wurrung, comprising a small group of elderly men and women, were living a partly traditional life at Mordialloc as well as selling ducks and eels. Benbow, a Boon Wurrung Arweet (clan leader), was travelling to Mordialloc when he died on 5 July 1852 at Green Point.

By the 1860s, Mordialloc became a popular recreational spot for settlers, offering bathing, fishing and hunting with new bridges and roads. The Aboriginal Protection Board decided to sell the reserve. Another Boon Wurrung clan leader, Derrimut, who had been a close friend of founding settler John Fawkner (see Site 19, p. 71), also lived at Mordialloc Reserve. With the assistance of Assistant Protector William Thomas, Derrimut advocated retaining the reserve including the Boon Wurrung burial grounds but they were unsuccessful. Derrimut's health deteriorated after the loss of the last of his country and he died in April 1864.

In 1866, parts of the reserve were sold for residential use beside the beach as the first Long Beach Allotments. The last known resident, Jimmy Dunbar, passed away in April 1877. A year later the Mechanics Institute, later the Court House, was constructed on the reserve lands.

Numerous shell middens and scarred trees have been found in the park and adjacent to Mordialloc Creek. Today the park continuously flies the Aboriginal flag to commemorate the former reserve.

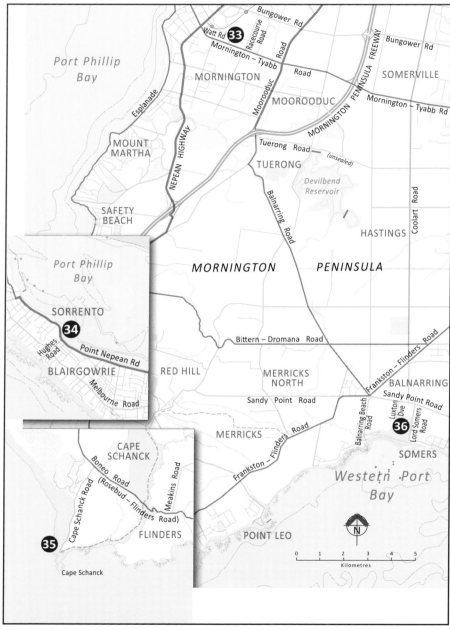

Sites 33–36.

Mornington Peninsula. Photograph by James Lauritz, courtesy Tourism Victoria.

MORNINGTON PENINSULA

Mornington Peninsula is a 720-square-kilometre boot-shaped promontory separating Port Phillip and Western Port, just over an hour's drive south from the city centre. It is the most popular recreation area near Melbourne with coastal trails through national parks, green hinterlands and wild ocean beaches, farms and favoured towns by the sea.

It was also the home of the Boon Wurrung people for many thousands of years and where they first encountered the arrival of Europeans. Food was plentiful with abundant marsupials, seafood and edible plants. There is intense archaeological evidence of their occupation along the coast with middens and evidence of more permanent camps. There was also an extensive network of pathways created by seasonal journeys for social, hunting, trading and spiritual purposes.

SITES

Top: *Tarnuk* by Robert Kelly.
Right: Inside the Baluk Arts gallery.

DESCRIPTION

Baluk Arts is a group of experienced and emerging Aboriginal artists based in Mornington. It displays and sells Indigenous art, provides facilities for artists, and delivers workshops on Indigenous art.

LOCATION

6 Bruce Street, Mornington. Melway: 145 J3.

HOURS

Tuesdays to Saturdays from 10am–5pm.

TIME 30 minutes.

FURTHER INFORMATION

Tel: (03) 5975 5000
Web: www.balukarts.org.au

SITE 33
Baluk Arts

Baluk Arts was created in 2009 by Aboriginal artists from Frankston, the Mornington Peninsula and southeast Melbourne. *Baluk* is a local Boon Wurrung word meaning clan or extended family group. The not-for-profit organisation provides facilities and support for artists to develop their skills and practice as well as providing the wider public with opportunities to experience Indigenous culture. Many artists are assisted to showcase their work in local, statewide or national exhibitions. Workshops, artists-in-residence and arts consultancy are provided as services to organisations, schools or events.

Through Baluk Arts, family groups and members of the Stolen Generations have reconnected with their culture and express their histories through artistic practice. Over 200 Aboriginal and Torres Strait Islander people from as far as Mordialloc, Dandenong, St Kilda and Wonthaggi have been connected through art practice with the Frankston and Mornington Peninsula community.

A wide range of locally made Aboriginal artworks including artefacts are on display and available for sale from the Baluk Arts Centre. An online shop is also available.

Former Collins Settlement site, Foreshore Reserve, Sullivan's Bay.

SITE 34
Collins Settlement

By the 1800s, the Boon Wurrung people had become increasingly aware of European visitors. Seven British and French expeditions reached Western Port between 1798 and 1826. However, it was the first official settlement on the Nepean Peninsula near Sorrento that marked the beginning of the end of the traditional Kulin way of life in Port Phillip. In 1803, Lieutenant-Colonel David Collins established a settlement of convicts, soldiers and settlers at Sullivan Bay to discourage French occupation and support the sealing industry. The small village dispossessed the Boonwurrung balug clan of an important willam.

Sullivans Bay lies between two hills called the Two Sisters. The settlement hospital was on the Western Sister, the administration on the Eastern Sister and the parade ground was in between (today the Foreshore Reserve and picnic ground). Thirty settlers died during the expedition and a Graves Reserve is located at the Eastern Sister.

In 1803, signs of Boon Wurrung occupation were so extensive that colonist William Crook, observed, 'One could scarcely

DESCRIPTION

The first European settlement in Port Phillip Bay at Sullivan Bay near Sorrento impacted heavily on an extensive Boon Wurrung habitation area. Middens are still visible today.

LOCATION

The Collins Historic Settlement site with Visitors Centre, Graves Reserve, Monument and Lookout is located ninety kilometres from Melbourne, off the Point Nepean Road, between Sorrento and Blairgowrie. Melway: 157 F to G10. The Foreshore Reserve and picnic ground is opposite Westmore Avenue. Melway: 157 F10.

GETTING THERE

Parking: Available at the site.

Public transport: Frankston Station and then bus number 78 to Westmore Avenue, Sorrento.

TIME Up to 1 hour.

FURTHER INFORMATION

For information about access to the Visitors Centre, contact:
Parks Victoria
Tel: 13 19 63
Web: www.parkweb.vic.gov.au

Right: Sullivan's Bay, Eastern Sister.

walk ten yards without meeting traces of the natives — their huts...but especially their fires. There were shells [middens] in great abundance underground in almost every part.'

The area still retains large middens showing extensive habitation on the Eastern Sister and the Foreshore Reserve. Some middens show more than one layer of occupation and are estimated to be up to 2000 years old.

A number of Boon Wurrung people were killed or wounded resisting European occupation. Prior to the Collins Settlement, a party led by Lieutenant Murray fired on a group near Sullivans Bay on 17 February 1802. Settlers also fired on people on at least three occasions and burned down their huts despite Collins' orders to prevent conflict. Confronting a lack of fresh water and Koorie hostility, Collins packed up in 1804 and sailed off to start an alternative settlement in Tasmania.

Following Collins' departure, the Boon Wurrung were still prey to attacks by roving sealers and whalers. In 1826, British and French expeditions had noted sealers living with Aboriginal women at Sealers Cove on Phillip Island (Western Port). In the 1820s and 1830s an estimated 20–50 women and children were abducted for use as slaves on sealing stations.

Yoni Yonka, sketch by George Henry Haydon. Sketch of relationships of encampments from the William Thomas papers 1834–1868, 1902, Mitchell Library. Reproduced with the permission of the State Library of New South Wales.

KIDNAPPING 1833

Members of today's Boon Wurrung community in Melbourne can trace their ancestry back to women who were kidnapped by seal and whale hunters and taken to Bass Strait islands. In 1837 colonial authorities were sufficiently alarmed by such reports to send Chief Protector George Robinson to visit the islands to locate the women including the wife of clan leader Derrimut.

Robertson was assisted by a Tasmanian Aboriginal woman Pyterruner (or Matilda) who had been a captive of sealers herself. Pyterruner described to Robinson how sealers led by a George Meredith had used her as a decoy to entice a group of Boon Wurrung women on a beach near Point Nepean who were then abducted by the men. Robertson and Pyterruner identified some women from Port Philip in Bass Strait but he was unsuccessful in arranging their return.

Pyterruner's story was confirmed by a young Boon Wurrung man who arrived by ship in Melbourne in 1841. His name was Yoni Yonka and he became well-known for his intelligence and command of English. He related that he had been abducted together with eight Boon Wurrung women as a boy. He later travelled in a vessel to Swan River where he worked for four years before travelling to Adelaide and working his passage back to Melbourne where he was emotionally reunited with his clan.

The kidnapping by lawless sealers and whalers of Aboriginal women would have had devastating effects on the wellbeing of the Kulin. Apart from the personal loss, women were the main economic providers for their families. Descendants of the removed women in recent years have returned to Victoria and research continues today to trace the family connections of those affected by these and other abductions.

DESCRIPTION

Bunjil's Cave is a stalactite cave at Cape Schanck Reserve associated with the Kulin creator ancestor.

LOCATION

420 Cape Schanck Road, Cape Schanck, ninety minutes south of Melbourne at the southern end of the Mornington Peninsula. Melway: 257 F12.

GETTING THERE

It is a thirty minute walk to the cave from the Cape Schanck Reserve car park. Access to the cave is limited as it has can only be approached at very low tides and the reef platform can experience large unexpected waves. Advice should always be sought from Parks Victoria rangers.

HOURS

The kiosk closes around 4pm.

FACILITIES

The reserve car park has public toilets and picnic tables. There are two walks to lookouts and to the beach, with spectacular scenery. A popular 2.6km track also goes to Bushrangers Bay.

ADMISSION

Free. Entry fees only apply for the 1859 lightstation precinct including the lighthouse, museum and former lighthouse keeper's residence.

Entrance to Bunjil's Cave. Courtesy Flinders District Historical Society.

SITE 35
Bunjil's Cave

Bunjil's Cave, also known as Angel Cave, is a stalactite cave located on the foreshore below Cape Schanck Lighthouse and Reserve. According to a Dreaming story, Bunjil, the creator being in the form of a wedge-tailed eagle, took shelter in this cave during a storm. In 1846, William Hull, a well-known resident of Melbourne described it:

> This cavern, facing the sea, they say was once the residence of Pungil, the God of the natives, who they believe came out of the sea — formed it, and much delighted in it. There are no paintings or marks, but apparently a wide altar and decayed steps in the recess.

Lookouts from the 80 metre high cliffs above the cave offer spectacular views over ancient geological formations called Pulpit Rock and the Devils Desk, formed over millions of years. Here, you can sense the power of wind, wave and stone. This wild and pristine coastline, dominated by sand dunes, cliffs, headlands, shore platforms and reefs is a suitable setting for the home of the ancestral creator of the Kulin people.

Bunjil's Cave is a heritage protected site in the clan estate of the Boonwurrung balug. Access is difficult as it only be approached from the beach at very low tides and the reef platform can be subject to large unexpected waves.

Caves and sink holes featured in many stories of Aboriginal people as the place of dangerous spirits, ancestral heroes, or important in the movement of souls to their resting places.

Overnight accommodation can be booked in the lightstation. Tel: 1300 885 259 or (03) 5988 6184.

TIME 1–2 hours.

FURTHER INFORMATION

Parks Victoria
Tel: 13 19 63
Web: www.parkweb.vic.gov.au

CONSIDERATIONS

Observe all fence security and signs. All Aboriginal cultural places and their artefacts in Victoria are protected by law.

READ ABOUT

BUNJIL THE ANCESTRAL CREATOR

For the Kulin, Bunjil, the wedge-tailed eagle, is a creator deity, culture hero and ancestral being and one of two moiety ancestors, the other being the cunning crow called Waarn (Waa). Bunjil keeps a watchful eye on people and offers guidance to those who choose to listen. He has two wives and a son, Binbeal the rainbow. His brother is Balayang the bat. He is assisted by six powerful young men who represent the clans of the wedge-tailed eagle moiety: Djurt-djurt the Nankeen Kestrel, Thara the quail hawk, Yukope the parakeet, Dantum the parrot, Tadjeri the brushtail possum and Turnong the gliding possum.

Bunjil gathered his wives and sons together after creating the mountains, rivers, all living things, and the laws for humans to live by. He then asked Waarn, who had charge of the winds, to open his bags and let out some wind. Waarn opened a bag in which he kept his whirlwinds, creating a storm which uprooted huge trees. But Bunjil asked for even stronger wind. Waarn opened all his bags, and Bunjil and his people were blown upwards into the sky. Bunjil himself became the star Altair and his two wives, the black swans, became stars on either side.

Bunjil is also associated with a cave or chasm in eastern Melbourne recorded by Robert Brough Smyth in 1878. It was located in Cave Hill quarry near today's Cave Hill Road, Lilydale. Bunjil made this deep hole when he was angry with the Yarra or Wurundjeri people for committing misdeeds. He caused a star to fall to the earth, striking and killing a great many people. The impact of this falling star created Buk-ker-tillible, a chasm deep into the earth. In fact the Kulin described Buk-ker-tillible as having no bottom. When stones were thrown into it, they were never heard to land.

According to Kulin stories, Bunjil also sheltered in a cave in western Victoria, in the Black Range State Park. This site called Bunjil's Shelter is a well-known visitor attraction and contains the only known rock art painting of Bunjil.

MORNINGTON PENINSULA

Above: Coolart Wetlands.

SITE 36
Coolart Wetlands and Homestead

Within four years of settlement, the Boon Wurrung people were alarmed to find their territory on the Mornington Peninsula being rapidly sold up for grazing runs. They requested permanent land that they could call their own from Assistant Protector William Thomas.

On 23 December 1839, Thomas enthusiastically passed on their request. He pointed out that the Boon Wurrung had nowhere else to go. In June 1840, Thomas announced good news to the clans — he had received approval for them to select a reserve of ten square miles of land. The delighted Boon Wurrung chose Kullurk (also spelled Coolart and Colourt), today's Sandy Point, as a permanent home. Thomas heartily approved of their choice. The site had abundant fresh water and wildlife.

However, on 28 July 1840, Chief Protector George Robinson ordered Thomas to remove the Boon Wurrung from Kullurk. Robinson insisted that they share a reserve with the Woiwurrung at Nerre Nerre Warren. The Boon Wurrung were bitterly disappointed and some of them blamed Thomas for many years. He continued to camp with them at different protectorate stations around

Mornington called Tubberubbabel (Port Arthur), Kangerong and Buckkermitterwarrer (beside today's Dromana Drive-in cinema) but he believed that none were as suitable as Kullurk. Ten years later he was still discussing a permanent reserve with the governor but he was pessimistic:

> '…the startling fact that not one-third of their number exist which at my first coming among them numbered but eighty-three, cannot leave more than twenty-eight. I fear there are less, and no children to fill up the ranks of the dead, points the dial of mortality to steadily to their speedy extinction — taking these considerations into account it would be useless sacrificing a great block of land for this tribe.'

Today, Kullurk (Coolart Wetlands and Homestead) is a popular public estate with a homestead built by Frederick Grimwade in 1895. The eighty-seven hectares of grounds are close by the sea and occupied by wetlands, a wildlife sanctuary, woodlands and gardens with over sixty species of birds. It is easy to see why almost seven generations ago, the Boon Wurrung saw it as the most precious part of their traditional lands.

Marie Fels details this story in her e-book, *I Succeeded Once: the Aboriginal Protectorate on the Mornington Peninsula, 1839–1840.*

OTHER ACTIVITIES

Coolart is famed for bird watching including Minsmere Hide.

FURTHER INFORMATION

Parks Victoria
Tel: 13 19 63
Web: www.parkweb.vic.gov.au

Coolart Wetlands.

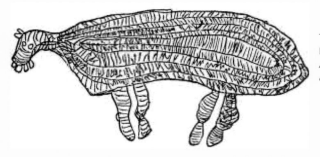

This drawing was made by a Murray River Aboriginal person in 1848. After Brough Smyth, *The Aborigines of Victoria*, i. 437, Fig. 245.

BUNYIPS AT TOORADIN

Traditional Aboriginal beliefs describe the existence of a class of non-human, indestructible and all powerful beings responsible for sickness and supernatural events. One of these beings called the Too-roe-dun (Bunyip), lived in a deep waterhole at the mouth of Sawtells Creek at Tooradin. The Bunyip seized and devoured anyone who ventured too close. Today this area is adjacent to a foreshore reserve with picnic grounds, play areas and views of French Island.

Sawtells Creek is an outlet to Western Port of the former Koo-wee-rup swamp. The Bunyip also lived in this swamp which was once a vast wetland that provided a wide range of native plants and animals for the Mayune balug clan of the Boon Wurrung people. A view over the former swamp can be obtained from the Swamp Lookout Tower at the Bunyip River picnic ground, a few kilometres further east of Tooradin.

Bunyip stories have been retold in a variety of Australian literature, film and language since the nineteenth century. Scientists have suggested that descriptions may stem from memories of extinct gigantic marsupial or seals making their way up inland rivers. William Buckley, an escaped convict from Sullivans Bay in 1803, lived for thirty-two years with the Wathaurong people west of Geelong. In his 1852 narrative he described bunyips in Lake Modewarre and other inland lakes:

'[a] very extraordinary amphibious animal, which the natives call Bunyip…I could never see any part, except the back, which appeared to be covered with feathers of a dusky grey colour. It seemed to be about the size of a full grown calf.

Another fearful creature occurred in Kulin creation stories. Its name was Mindye, and it was a huge snake of immense length and power. In 1840, Mindye was called forth by Wirriraps (Aboriginal healers), to wreak revenge on the settlers in Melbourne for a mass arrest of Aboriginal people (see Site 20, p. 73).

Two of the last known Boon Wurrung people in the Western Port area, Jimmy Dunbar and his wife Nancy, were employed at Harewood House in Tooradin, in 1875. They later moved to the Mordialloc Aboriginal Reserve.

Location: The mouth of Sawtells Creek Inlet in Tooradin is now an attractive estuary with picnic grounds, play areas, and views of French Island. Melway: 144 A6.

LIST OF ORGANISATIONS

A number of places in Melbourne offer opportunities to learn more about Aboriginal heritage. A selection of these is provided below in alphabetical order.

Baluk Arts
6 Bruce Street
Mornington VIC 3931
Tel: (03) 5975 5000
Web: www.balukarts.org.au

Boon Wurrung Foundation
208 Bank Street
South Melbourne VIC 3205
Tel: (03) 9682 9578
Web: www.boonwurrung.org

Bunjilaka Aboriginal Cultural Centre
Museum Victoria
11 Nicholson Street
Carlton VIC 3053
Tel: 1300 135 858
Web: www.museumvictoria.com.au/bunjilaka
Email: bunjilaka@museum.vic.gov.au

Bunurong Land and Sea Association Inc.
PO Box 96
Cockatoo VIC 3781
Tel: 0400 530 060
Email: bunurong@dcsi.net.au

Bunurong Land Council Aboriginal Corporation
370 Thenis Street
Pakenham VIC 3810
Tel: (03) 5678 0250
Email: bunurong@dcsi.net.au

Dandenong & District Aborigines Co-Operative Ltd
3 Carroll Avenue
Dandenong VIC 3175
Tel: (03) 9794 5933
Web: www.ddacl.org.au

Enmaraleek Jerrang Association Inc.
9 Central Grove
Broadmeadows VIC 3047
Tel: (03) 9302 2742

The Ian Potter Centre
National Gallery of Victoria Australia
Federation Square, The Atrium
Melbourne VIC 3000
Tel: (03) 8620 2222
Web: www.ngv.vic.gov.au

ILBIJERRI Theatre Company
5 Blackwood Street
North Melbourne VIC 3051
Tel: (03) 9329 9097
Web: www.ilbijerri.com.au
Email: info@ilbijerri.com.au

3KND Kool N Deadly (Radio Station)
48–56 Mary St, Preston VIC 3072
Tel: (03) 9471 1305
Web: www.3knd.org.au

Koorie Heritage Trust
295 King Street
Melbourne VIC 3000
Tel: (03) 8622 2600
Web: www.koorieheritagetrust.com
Email: info@koorieheritagetrust.com

Koorie Records Unit
Public Record Office of Victoria
99 Shiel Street
North Melbourne VIC 3051
Tel: (03) 9348 5600
Web: www.prov.vic.gov.au
Email: koorie.records@prov.vic.gov.au

Melbourne Visitor Centre
Federation Square
Corner Swanston and Flinders streets
Melbourne VIC 3000
Tel: (03) 9658 9658
Web: www.thatsmelbourne.com.au

Mirimbiak Nations Aboriginal Corporation
75–79 Chetwynd Street
North Melbourne VIC 3051
Tel: (03) 9326 3900

National Native Title Tribunal (Melbourne office)
Level 6, Commonwealth Law Courts Building
305 William Street
Melbourne VIC 3000
Tel: 1800 640 501 or (03) 9920 3000
Web: www.nntt.gov.au
Email: vicandtasenquiries@nntt.gov.au

Office of Aboriginal Affairs Victoria
Level 9, 1 Spring Street
Melbourne VIC 3000
Tel: 1800 762 003
Web: www.dpc.vic.gov.au
Email: Aboriginalaffairs@dpc.vic.gov.au

Reconciliation Victoria
Hub Melbourne, Level 3
673 Bourke Street
Melbourne VIC 3000
Tel: (03) 9016 0657
Web: www.reconciliationvic.org.au
Email: info@reconciliationvic.org.au

Victorian Aboriginal Corporation for Languages
295 King Street
Melbourne VIC 3000
Tel: 1300 973 697 or (03) 9600 3811
Web: www.vaclang.org.au
Email: info@vaclang.org.au

Victorian Aboriginal Heritage Council
Office of Aboriginal Affairs Victoria
Level 9, 1 Spring Street
Melbourne VIC 3000
Tel: (03) 9208 3243
Web: www.dpc.vic.gov.au
Email: VAHC@dpc.vic.gov.au

LIST OF ORGANISATIONS

Wurundjeri Tribe Land Cultural Heritage Council Inc.
1st Floor, Providence Building
Abbotsford Convent
1 St Heliers Street
Abbotsford VIC 3067
Tel: (03) 8673 0901
Email: reception@wurundjeri.com.au

GLOSSARY

Arweet (clan leader)

baluk/balluk/bulag (people/clan name). Usage varies depending on context

Birrarung (name of Yarra River)

branjep (men's 'aprons')

Gageed (ceremony to dispel sickness)

Gayip/Gaggip (ceremony to strengthen bonds of unity/ friendship)

gombert (reed necklace)

ilbi-jerri (nosepeg)

jibauk (initiation ceremony)

mangurt (ball)

Marngrook (game)

miam (shelter)

moogji (friends)

murnong (yam tubers)

Ngargee (corroboree)

Ngurungaeta (clan leader)

Tanderrum (ceremony of hospitality & friendship)

wadi (club)

willam (camp, place)

Wirrarap (healer/medicine man)

wurrung (language group)

REFERENCE LIST

Baluk Arts 2011, *Baluk Wurrung: stories from Aboriginal people in South East Melbourne*, Rosebud, Melbourne.

Barwick, DE 1984, 'Mapping the Past: An Atlas of Victorian Clans 1835–1904, Part 1', *Aboriginal History*, vol. 8, no. 2, pp. 100–31.

—— 1998, *Rebellion at Coranderrk*, Aboriginal History Inc., Canberra.

Bennett, C 1990, Queen Victoria Market J Shed: Archaeological Investigation Reports. Report on the Human Skeletal Remains from the Queen Victoria Market, unpublished report to the City of Melbourne. Recorded by: S. Lavelle.

Berg, J & Faulkhead, S 2010, *Power and passion: our ancestors return home*, Koorie Heritage Trust Inc., Melbourne.

Billot, CP 1979, *John Batman: the story of John Batman and the founding of Melbourne*, Hyland House, Melbourne.

—— (ed.) 1982, *Melbourne's missing chronicle: being the journal of preparations for departure to and proceedings at Port Phillip by John Pascoe Fawkner*, Quartet Books, Melbourne.

Biosis Research 1999, Aboriginal heritage study: report to the City of Maribyrnong as part of the Maribyrnong Heritage Review, City of Maribyrnong, Melbourne.

Boyce, J 2013, *1835: The Founding of Melbourne and the Conquest of Australia*, Black Inc. Melbourne.

Brown, S & Lane, S 1997, *Brimbank City Council Aboriginal cultural heritage study — background document*, report to the City of Brimbank, Brimbank.

Bride, TF (ed.) 1969, *Letters from Victorian pioneers*, William Heineman Ltd, Melbourne.

Broome, R 2005, *Aboriginal Victorians: a history since 1800*, Allen & Unwin, Crows Nest NSW.

Cannon, M (ed) 1983, 'Aborigines and Protectors, 1838–39', *Historical Records of Victoria*, vol. 2B, Public Record Office, Melbourne.

Christie, MF 1979, *Aborigines in colonial Victoria, 1835–86*, Sydney University Press, Sydney.

Clark, ID 1990, 'Aboriginal Languages and Clans, an historical atlas of western and central Victoria, 1800–1900', *Monash Publications in Geography*.

—— 2001, *The Yalukit-willam: the first people of the City of Hobsons Bay*, City of Hobsons Bay, Altona.

—— & Heydon, TA 2004, *A bend in the Yarra: a history of the Merri Creek Protectorate Station and Merri Creek Aboriginal School 1841–1851*, Aboriginal Studies Press, Canberra.

—— & Kostanski, LM 2007, *An Indigenous history of the City of Stonnington, Final Report*, University of Ballarat, Ballarat.

—— (ed.) 2000a, *The Journals of George Augustus Robinson, Chief Protector, Port Phillip Aboriginal Protectorate, 1839–1852*, 6 vols, Heritage Matters, Clarendon.

—— (ed.) 2000b, *The Papers of George Augustus Robinson, Chief Protector, Port Phillip Aboriginal Protectorate*, vol. 2, Heritage Matters.

Cooper, JB 1931, *The history of St. Kilda from its first settlement to a city and after, 1840 to 1930*, 2 vols, St. Kilda City Council, Melbourne.

Coutts, JF 1981, *Victoria's first official settlement: Sullivan Bay, Port Phillip,. Victoria archaeological survey*, Ministry for Conservation, Port Phillip.

Daly, C 1925, 'Reminiscences from 1841 of William Kyle: a pioneer', *Victorian Historical Magazine*, vol. 10, no. 3, p. 165.

Dixon, R & Blake, B (eds) 1991, *The Aboriginal Language of Melbourne and Other Grammatical Sketches*, vol. 4, Oxford University Press, South Melbourne.

Dunstan, K 1998, *The paddock that grew: the story of the Melbourne Cricket Club*, Century Hutchinson, Australia.

Eidelson, M 2014, *Walks in Port Phillip: A guide to the cultural landscapes of a city*, City of Port Phillip, Port Phillip.

Faulkhead, S & Berg, J et al 2010, *Power and the Passion: Our Ancestors Return Home*, Koorie Heritage Trust, Melbourne.

Fels, M 1988, *Good men and true, the Aboriginal Police of the Port Phillip District, 1837–1853*, Melbourne University Press, Melbourne.

—— 2011, *I Succeeded Once: the Aboriginal Protectorate on the Mornington Peninsula 1839–1840*, ANU E Press, Canberra.

Flood, J 1989, *Archaeology of the Dreamtime: the story of prehistoric Australia and her people*, Collins, Sydney.

Frankel, D 1991, *Remains to be seen: archaeological insights into Australian prehistory*, Longman Cheshire, Melbourne.

Garryowen 1888, *The chronicles of early Melbourne, 1835 to 1852: historical, anecdotal and personal*, ed. E Finn, La Trobe University, Melbourne.

Goulding, M & Menis, M 2006, Moreland post-contact Aboriginal heritage study, prepared for Moreland City Council by Goulding Heritage Consulting Pty Ltd.

Griffin, D, Freedman, DL, Nicholson Jnr, B, McConachie, F & Parmington, A 2013l, 'The Koorong Project: experimental archaeology and Wurundjeri continuation of cultural practices', in Excavations, Surveys and Heritage Management in Victoria, Voume 2, Susan Lawrence, David Frankel, Caroline Spry Shaun Canningllya Berelov (eds), p. 63.

Howitt, AW 1904, *The native tribes of south-east Australia*, Macmillan and Co., London.

Jones, VJ 1983, *Solomons Ford*, Globe Press, Fitzroy.

Keeler, C & Couzens, V 2010, Meerreeng-an here is my country: the story of Aboriginal Victoria told through art, Koorie Heritage Trust, Melbourne.

Land, C 2014, *Tunnerminnerwait and Maulboyheenner: The involvement of Aboriginal people from Tasmania in key events of early Melbourne*, City of Melbourne, Melbourne.

Lemon, A 1983, *The Northcote side of the river*, Hargreen Publishing [for the] City of Northcote, Melbourne.

Massola, A 1968, *Bunjil's cave: myths, legends and superstitions of the Aborigines of south-east Australia*, Lansdowne, Melbourne.

McBryde, I 1978, 'Wil-im-ee Moor-ring Or, where do axes come from?: stone axe distribution and exchange patterns in Victoria', *Mankind*, vol. 11, no. 3, pp. 354–82.

McCrae, H (ed.) 1992, *Georgiana's journal*, Angus and Robertson, Melbourne.

Mulvaney, DJ 1970, 'Green Gully revisited: the later excavations', *Memoirs of the National Museum of Victoria*, vol. 30, pp. 79–92.

Nani G & James, A 2013, *Coranderrk: We Will Show the Country*, Aboriginal Studies Press, Canberra.

Pepper, P & De Araugo, T 1985, *What did happen to the Aborigines of Victoria, Vol. 1, The Kurnai of Gippsland*, Hyland House, Melbourne.

Presland, G 2010, *First people: the eastern Kulin of Melbourne, Port Phillip and Central Victoria*, Museum Victoria, Melbourne.

Rae-Ellis, V 1996, *Black Robinson: Protector of Aborigines*, Melbourne University Press, Melbourne.

Rhodes D 1990a, *The Dandenong police paddocks: an archaeological survey*, Aboriginal Affairs Victoria, Melbourne.

Roberts, J 1986, *Jack of Cape Grim: a Victorian adventure*, Greenhouse Publications, Richmond, Vic.

Romanov-Hughes, A 2007, 'Batman Treaty Memorial Located', *Northcote Leader*, 3 July, viewed on 3 June 2013, <http://pandora.nla.gov.au/pan/15195/20090125-0008/home.vicnet.net.au/_pioneers/pppg5be.html>.

Select Committee of the Legislative Council on the Aborigines 1858–9, *Report of the Select Committee of the Legislative Council on the Aborigines*, John Ferres, Government Printer, Melbourne.

Shaw, AGL 1996, *A history of the Port Phillip district Victoria before separation*, Melbourne University Press, Melbourne.

Smythe, RB 1972 (1876), *The Aborigines of Victoria: with notes relating to the habits of the natives of other parts of Australia and Tasmania*, John Currey O'Neill, Melbourne.

Webb, C 1995, *The identification and documentation of silcrete quarries*, Heritage Services Branch, Aboriginal Affairs Victoria, Melbourne.

Wiencke, S 1984, *When the wattles bloom again: the life and times of William Barak, last chief of the Yarra Yarra tribe*, Shirley W. Wiencke, Woori Yallock, Vic.

Zola, N & Gott, B 1992, *Koori plants, Koori people: traditional Aboriginal food, fibre and healing plants of Victoria*, Koori Heritage Trust, Melbourne.

INDEX

Note, page numbers in *italics* indicate photographs or artworks.

First published in 1997 by Aboriginal Studies Press

Second edition published in 2014 by Aboriginal Studies Press

© Australian Institute of Aboriginal and Torres Strait Islander Studies

Aboriginal Studies Press is the publishing arm of the Australian Institute of Aboriginal and Torres Strait Islander Studies.

GPO Box 553, Canberra, ACT 2601
Phone: (61 2) 6246 1183
Fax: (61 2) 6261 4288
Email: asp@aiatsis.gov.au
Web: www.aiatsis.gov.au/asp

A Cataloguing-in-Publication entry is available from the National Library of Australia
www.trove.nla.gov.au
ISBN 9781922059710 (pb)
ISBN 9781922059727 (PDF ebook)

All information in this publication was correct at time of printing. Events, exhibitions and admission fees at cultural institutions are subject to change and it may be necessary to verify details with the relevant organisations before visiting. The publisher has made every effort to contact copyright owners for permission to use material reproduced in this book. If your material has been used inadvertently without permission, please contact the publisher immediately.

Cultural consultation has been undertaken with the Wurundjeri Cultural Consultation Committee of Elders and the Boon Wurrung Foundation.

Maps by Brenda Thornley. Base maps © Melway Publishing Pty Ltd.

All photographs by the author unless otherwise noted.

Front cover: (top left) *Scar: A Stolen Vision art installation*, photograph by Hari Ho; (top middle) *Bunjil*, artist Bruce Armstrong; (top right) Tanderrum ceremony, presented by Melbourne Festival, Ilbijerri Theatre Company in association with The Bardas Family Foundation, photograph by Bindi Cole; (bottom left) 'A corroboree of the Aboriginal Australians', engraving, Calvert Samuel, 1867, State Library of Victoria, IMP27/07/67/10; (bottom right) William Cooper, street art [artist unknown].

Back cover: (left) Webb (Eel Trap) Bridge, artist Robert Owen, architects Denton Corker Marshall; (right) *Gayip*, artists Nadim Karam and Mandy Nicholson.

Border artwork: Detail from *Coranderrk*, Mandy Nicholson.

Printed in Australia by McPherson's Printing Group

FSC
www.fsc.org
MIX
Paper from
responsible sources
FSC® C011613